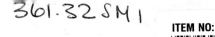
ITEM NO: 19

KT-452-174

The Heart of the Night

Out of hours crisis intervention in health and social care: The work of Social Services Emergency Duty Teams

Martin Smith

RHP

Russell House Publishing

First published in 2004 by
Russell House Publishing Ltd.
4 St. George's House
Uplyme Road
Lyme Regis
Dorset DT7 3LS

Tel: 01297-443948
Fax: 01297-442722
e-mail: help@russellhouse.co.uk
www.russellhouse.co.uk

British Library Cataloguing-in-publication Data:
A catalogue record for this book is available from the British Library.

ISBN: 1-903855-30-6

Typeset by TW Typesetting, Plymouth, Devon
Printed by Arrowsmith, Bristol
Cover artwork by Jonathan Smith

About Russell House Publishing

RHP is a group of social work, probation, education and youth and
community work practitioners and academics working in collaboration with
a professional publishing team.
Our aim is to work closely with the field to produce innovative and valuable
materials to help managers, trainers, practitioners and students.
We are keen to receive feedback on publications and new ideas for
future projects.
For details of our other publications please visit our website or ask us for a
catalogue. Contact details are on this page.

For some must watch while some must sleep, Thus runs the world away

(Shakespeare)

*One does not become enlightened by imagining figures of light, but by
making the darkness conscious*

(C.G. Jung)

*All human beings have certain common basic needs: physical, emotional,
intellectual, social and spiritual. In adverse circumstances these common
needs are felt with a special poignancy*

(F.P. Biestek)

Contents

Preface

Social services emergency duty teams (EDTs) have been at the forefront of providing and co-ordinating health and social care services for people of all ages out of usual office hours for nearly thirty years. Despite this, up until now, there has not been a concerted attempt to gather together in one volume a representation of the difficulties these teams face, the satisfactions they experience and the relationships they engage in. This book is an attempt to address this deficit.

The book begins charting the evolution of EDTs and considers the motivations of those who work in them. Ways in which work is organised and prioritised are illustrated. Chapter 1 establishes a pattern for later chapters by ending with a series of recommendations intended to promote best practice. After this introductory chapter the next three chapters are primarily concerned with practice issues. Those with particular interests in working with children, mental health problems and vulnerable adults will be able to find a specific consideration of each of these groups in Chapters 2, 3 and 4. The following three chapters address primarily management concerns as training (given and received), health and safety issues and support for workers are discussed. Chapters 8 and 9 set the work in a broader focus as partnership working and customer satisfaction, two crucial constituents of work in health and social care today, are illustrated and debated. As most peoples' lives move to embrace a 'twenty-four hour culture' Chapter 10 looks ahead to the future and speculates as to the contributions EDTs might make as services available out of hours increase and expand. While looking forward this chapter also looks back on themes which have recurred throughout the preceding chapters as crucially underpinning crisis work out of normal office hours; assuming (or being forced into) a parental role, the pervading importance of attachment theory, the value of working in the short-term and the need to retain the good things from the past while embracing potentially helpful innovations suggested by the future.

This book is intended for two main readerships. As Chapter 5 makes clear out of hours services offer many rich learning opportunities for those undertaking qualifying and post-qualifying courses in health and social care settings. EDT workers have developed sophisticated and effective partnership agreements with other agencies working through the 'twilight hours', their assessment skills are finely honed, they are challenged to respond quickly, effectively and safely and have to cultivate the skill of thinking 'on their feet'. They need to distinguish the 'genuine' from the apparent, yet not real emergency, they need to be concerned enough about what they are faced with but not so concerned that thinking becomes impossible. These are crucial skills for students to discover. This book is therefore intended to help them embark upon this journey. Secondly, many EDT workers have been providing high quality, efficient, effective and (often) appreciated responses to people in distress for decades. The value of this work has often gone largely unrecognised. My hope is that this book will go some small way to acknowledging and illustrating the contribution made by EDTs and others who have provided out of hours services over the years and that they too will appreciate seeing the many different aspects of their work brought together under one title. For too long EDTs have been 'out of sight and out of mind'. As services increasingly expand into working beyond nine to five I hope the wealth of experience that EDT workers have accumulated when responding to those in crisis in the darkest hours will be appreciated. If it is, the extent of the contribution that these workers can make to the debates about what *works* for people in need is more likely to be realised. This book is therefore also for those experienced workers and planners with an interest in the development, current and future functioning of EDTs.

Martin Smith.

Acknowledgements

Sheila, Robert, Jonathan and Verity have provided good company, belief, fun, necessary commitment and welcome diversion throughout the writing of this book. Jean Nursten and Linnet McMahon helped inspire, protect and nurture my relationship with the writing process and Patrick McGrath and Andrew Cooper facilitated belief in this. Maria Ruegger provided vital inspiration for the book in its formative stages and was constantly encouraging throughout. Kay Clymo was extremely generous with her time, offering invaluable editorial advice and suggestions. Robert Johns, Christina Anderson and Rebecca Graham made helpful comments on the text and gave sustaining support throughout its writing. Many other colleagues and service users have contributed to this work in countless ways over the years. For these 'nameless acts of kindness', forgotten and remembered, much thanks. Thanks also to the journal *Practice* published by the *British Association of Social Workers* in which versions of chapters one, two, three, four, five and nine have been published previously.

Introduction

CHAPTER 1

Working at night: out of sight, out of mind?

This chapter begins with a review of the origins and subsequent evolution of Emergency Duty Teams (EDTs) in social services departments. Motivations of those who are attracted to work in an EDT are considered, as is the way in which work is organised. EDT workers face constantly changing challenges, and examples of these are provided and discussed. Consideration is given to how good working practice can be optimised between EDTs, partner agencies and daytime social work teams, and recommendations are suggested.

Origins and evolution of EDTs

Emergency Duty Teams (EDTs) were established by many local authority social services departments in the late 1970s. Previously, responses to crises arising out of office hours had been made by the same staff who worked daytime hours. Industrial action in some inner city departments drew attention to the demands that working long hours imposed on workers, causing questions to be asked about the quality of a service provided by 'a reluctant and dissatisfied staff' (O'Hagan, 1986: 10). While some parts of Great Britain still do provide an out of hours service by drawing on daytime workers these are now in the minority. The Social Services Inspectorate (SSI) commented in 1999, 'EDTs became the norm by the eighties and have remained so' (Department of Health, 1999a: 9). A similar recognition of the limitations of a system requiring individuals to provide a consistently good quality service if working day, night and weekends, along with the associated strain on personal and domestic life, has led to many general practitioners (GPs) combining together in collectives to provide out of hours cover for their patients in recent years. By doing this individual GPs have to be on cover less often, albeit for a larger area. This is likely to result in an easing of the cumulative stresses and strains that result from working too many hours, an improvement in the quality of service given, and a more predictable, balanced and satisfying life – personally and professionally.

The minority of areas which still use daytime workers to provide an out of hours response do so by way of a 'co-ordinator and runner (or responder)' system. A co-ordinator takes initial calls, often at their home. They then decide whether a situation can be dealt with on the telephone by offering listening, discussion, guidance, advice, brief counselling, referral on or by screening out inappropriate calls. Some 85–93 per cent of calls to EDTs can be dealt with in this way. If a response over the telephone is not sufficient, however, the co-ordinator may need to ask a 'runner' to visit, interview and assess. Because social work roles have become increasingly specialised over recent years, more than one runner needs to be available. A daytime social worker approved to assess service users under the Mental Health Act 1983 is unlikely to have the detailed knowledge and skills necessary to assess a child protection situation and vice-versa. In addition, emergency respite care may need to be provided for an older person whilst adults or children may need the presence of an 'appropriate adult' (Police and Criminal Evidence Act 1984) before they can interviewed. Co-ordinator and runner systems typically operate in areas where there is an established tradition of working in this way, the daytime staff welcome it (in some areas there is a waiting list to join the EDT) and there are sufficient people available to prevent any one worker having to be on duty too often or for excessive periods.

Nevertheless, in most areas of Great Britain out of hours cover is now provided by EDT social workers working from home or from an office base as part of a team. Often with only one or two workers on duty at any one time, EDTs typically cover at least 131 of the 168 hours that make up each week (78 per cent). The structures, systems and frameworks that operate in the day are not available at night thus the EDT worker has to work with considerable autonomy but with the frequent disadvantage of no readily available support. Clifford and Williams (2002) comment:

> . . . throughout Britain it is likely that the smallest number of social workers is dealing with the highest ratio of referrals, in the most 'hazardous' circumstances, with the most 'dangerous' service users, yet with the least professional, personal and administrative support . . . EDT intervention (is therefore likely to be) based on minimal information, minimal discussion, minimal support (for the worker) but may have maximum impact for the service user.
>
> (Clifford and Williams, 2002: 202)

Clifford and Williams also point out that despite the number of years during which EDTs have been covering at least 78 per cent of any working week and despite the quantity and complexity of work that they undertake, their operations and practices are only sparsely reported. Although there are indications that this is beginning to change (Smith and England, 1997; Smith et al., 1998; Smith, 1999a, 2000a, 2001a, 2001b) there is still comparatively little written about EDTs with only two pieces of systematic research published (Etherington and Parker, 1984; Clifford and Williams, 2002). Unless complaints and controversy arise there can be a tendency for senior managers not to feel a need to have a detailed knowledge of or involvement with their EDT provided that it enables them to sleep at night. EDT workers, often self-sufficient and enjoying their considerable autonomy, may themselves welcome the absence of managerial involvement and, on balance, prefer to be left alone. The first SSI report into EDTs in England in 1999 suggested that '. . . the (EDT) service has rarely had a high profile, and its development has been limited. In many departments, the out of hours service has been out of sight, and out of mind'. (DoH, 1999a: 1). In some ways this point is re-enforced by the fact that EDTs had not been reported upon by the SSI in England until 1999. The first equivalent inspection in Wales was published in 2001 (SSI for Wales, 2001).

The purpose of this book is to provide the reader with an insight into the workings of EDT social workers: what they do, how they cope, how they struggle. Examples are given of the wide-ranging crises that EDT workers respond to, from the apparently 'trivial' to the profoundly awful and tragic. Other professional and voluntary groups responding to crisis referrals both in and out of normal office hours, will find much that they recognise in the pages that follow. They will be able to reflect upon the issues discussed and the dilemmas exposed. Firstly, what motivates social workers to work in EDTs?

Motivations for working in EDTs

Most of the hours covered by social services EDTs are hours of darkness. Alvarez (1996: xiii) suggests there are reasons for being suspicious of people who choose to work while others sleep:

> . . . there is still something not quite right – maybe not even quite sane – about a working life led at night. There is something not quite right about nightlife, something shadowy in every sense. However efficiently artificial light annihilates the difference between night and day, it never wholly eliminates the primitive suspicion that night people are up to no good. They work under the cover of darkness because what they do cannot bear the scrutiny of day.

O'Hagan (1986: 11) argues for a more pragmatic motivation:

> Social workers join EDTs for a variety of reasons. Some may join to acquire or to exercise their experience and competence in crisis work, or to specialise in child care or mental health crisis. But there are sufficient grounds for suggesting a rather more powerful motivating factor: family and domestic commitments, more money, freedom and autonomy; generally, a good deal more convenient for the worker and his immediate family. There is nothing dubious about such motivation, nor should it be a point of criticism.

Although written some years ago O'Hagan's claims remain valid today. Additional motivational factors for working in EDTs can also be identified. Over recent years social workers have been required to specialise in particular areas of work with discrete service user groups. Throughout this same time EDT work has remained generic encompassing all aspects of social work provision; it thus suits those who prefer to work within a general rather than a specialist framework. EDT work can include the provision of a first line response to those in urgent need of money, food and housing in a way that daytime social work does not. This is because benefit agency and council offices are open by day and not by night and at weekends. While the advent of care management systems and the care programme approach have added to the bureaucratic form-filling aspects of social work, EDTs have been able, by and large, to avoid excessive paperwork. EDT workers will usually provide a brief narrative account of their involvement; this is faxed, telephoned or e-mailed to the relevant daytime office. Only essential paperwork needs completion. Even when such paperwork is completed there is often little, or sometimes no, information available to be included under prescribed headings. EDT workers spend comparatively little time in meetings compared with their daytime counter-parts. Typically about 90 per cent of their time can be made available to respond to calls from service users, whereas daytime colleagues can spend up to 30 or 40 per cent of their time in meetings of various kinds. Because there is no planned work, EDT workers arrive for a shift and need to respond to whatever comes in. What comes in can vary greatly, rather like an accident and emergency department of a hospital, where staff may be presented with needs ranging from a minor cut to a major heart attack.

A question often asked of EDT workers is, 'Don't you ever wonder what happened to X after your brief involvement?' While such wondering may be a feature of a minority of cases most EDT workers have come to EDTs following several years experience of working in daytime teams and are pleased to be free of the ongoing day-to-day responsibilities that this work entails. EDT workers do get paid more than their daytime colleagues. Usually this forms an additional percentage of salary for working 'unsocial hours'. This may provoke the question, 'Do you have to be an unsociable person to work unsocial hours?' While this may be an unfair charge to level at EDT workers, there are aspects of the work that are liable to attract people who like their own company and who relish or are resigned to having to respond to challenges alone. Some people may be attracted to joining EDTs as a form of rite of passage – a desire to prove growth and maturity – showing that they can face alone the worst the darkness holds and survive to tell the tale. Others may be attracted by driving to and from work on quieter roads since the times when their shifts start and finish will normally avoid rush hour traffic. There may be something about working when most other people are not working which changes the nature of the work and makes it seem less arduous and less *real*, less like work, somehow. In some senses the late night and early morning hours may even seem more *friendly* than the day. As Alvarez (1996: 259) puts it:

> . . . *after a certain point of no return, people even become friendlier, maybe because they are fewer, maybe because insomniacs have a freemasonry of their own and there is a companionship in being up and about while the rest of the world sleeps* . . .

Managers of EDTs tend also to continue to work on the rota and 'keep their hand in' by continuing to do the work while managing the team. In this they are likely to differ from daytime managers who tend to be less directly involved with service users as they concentrate on management rather than practice. Working in EDTs may be seen as a backwater, a haven, or being at the 'cutting edge' and 'heavy end'. Maybe it is a combination of all three. Whatever it is, the work needs to be organised.

Organisation of work in EDTs

An EDT worker will typically begin their weekday evening shift half an hour or so before daytime colleagues finish theirs, at around 5 p.m. This half an hour provides the opportunity for a hand-over of work. Daytime workers can telephone, e-mail or fax through details of work that may come to the attention of EDTs later that evening. EDTs often prefer a *brief* written summary of work already undertaken and reasons why the case in question may come to attention along with a recommended course of action to follow. Many teams have their own proforma that they ask daytime colleagues to complete. It is helpful if this brief written account is accompanied by an explanatory telephone call that can furnish further relevant context and detail. It is preferable that the referring worker completes the written summary so that names and addresses are spelt correctly. Sometimes hard-pressed daytime workers will call EDT, keen (even desperate, at times) to pass on their concerns and go home. They can be reluctant to complete paperwork, preferring to dictate what they want to say to the EDT worker taking the call. The EDT worker will resist this if at all possible since it is easy to mis-hear or misspell important place names that may be passed on hurriedly over the telephone.

On one occasion a concerned home carer telephoned to pass on her concern that a service user she had visited was not answering the door and she was worried about him. The EDT worker receiving the call asked the referrer to fax details in writing but she resisted this saying she was in a hurry and had no time to complete a written referral. She gave the name of his road which began with BR . . . As is customary in such cases the police were contacted and asked to check up on him. Some time later, the police called back to say that they had been unable to locate the road name given. It emerged that the road began with H rather than BR. The service user was found safe and well but the importance of getting significant details in writing or at least to verify the spellings of essential information was an important lesson.

A second reason for preferring written referrals is that there is often only one EDT worker available to receive referrals and having to write everything down can be an inefficient use of time if messages from other callers wanting attention are being recorded on the ansaphone meanwhile. Daytime workers may find it difficult to articulate verbal handovers of work as they are sometimes caught up in the tumultuous processes of work they are undertaking. They may not have been able to think through precisely, what it is that they want to pass on, what they want to say, or what outcomes they would like to achieve from doing so. Sometimes EDT workers feel that they are de-briefing daytime staff whilst attempting to reason out the nature of and reasons for the referrals they are making. Whereas daytime workers can be keen to detail *the story* of what has already happened, the EDT worker wants to know what daytime staff would like to be done should the service user come to attention out of hours. The role of EDT workers is often to carry out what the daytime worker would have done were they there to do it. Ideally they will make as few fundamental changes to any service user's life as possible. Policy statements usually commit EDTs to become involved only when situations cannot hold until the next working day.

In many teams a second EDT worker will often join the first worker an hour or two after the first worker has begun their shift. The two workers will then prioritise work in need of attention. It is highly unlikely, therefore, that any worker will leave the office base to make a visit until half an hour after the second worker's arrival. Because of the need to manage the work and staff in this way it is unhelpful for daytime colleagues to commit EDT workers to any timed appointments. Sometimes a daytime worker may telephone through to say, 'I've arranged for you to meet the doctors at the house at 6.30 p.m.'. While this may be done with the intention of being helpful it may well be counter-productive since the worker setting up the appointment cannot know what other work has also come into EDT that night. They can know only of their own referral and, while it may be understandable that they would prefer it to be given priority, it might be that other referrals are even more urgent. Work can be prioritised only when the relative needs of all referrals currently requiring attention are known as shown below.

Whilst taking referrals for one particular night, in the space of one hour the social worker was told of three Mental Health Act assessments requiring attention. The first concerned a service user currently held in a police station as a place of safety because he was thought to represent a danger to other people. The second was 35 miles away from the first where a man was said to be so disturbed that his relatives were sitting on him. The third was 20 miles away from the second (and 55 miles away from the first) and involved a service user out-patient in an accident and emergency department who was thought to be in danger of seriously harming herself. In addition to these three potential assessments there were requests for two child protection investigations and attendance at a police station to act as an appropriate adult under The Police and Criminal Evidence Act 1984.

At times like these it is necessary to decide which calls need responding to immediately and which can wait. Often these decisions are made in consultation with the police on the basis of anticipated danger or safety. Situations where people are thought to present the greatest risk of danger to themselves and/or others are accorded the highest priority. Completion of risk assessments aids this decision making (see Chapter 6).

The worker first on duty will finish their shift some six hours or so later leaving the second worker on duty through the night alone until daytime teams arrive for work at 9.00 a.m. The health and safety implications of having only one worker on duty through the early hours of the morning are discussed in Chapter 6. Although the cover provided by these one or two workers is minimal it is usually found to be sufficient. Such minimal teams continue to be used despite a general increase in the volume of work over recent years. One of the difficulties of providing appropriate staffing cover for EDTs is that such cover needs to be sufficient without being excessive. Planning for times of peak demand can be particularly problematic and to have a facility of calling on others to assist at particularly busy times is ideal. While the two workers on duty may both be constantly busy throughout some shifts (Smith and England, 1997) on quieter shifts neither may have much to do. This has led to suggestions that these quieter hours should be filled constructively. However, these hours are difficult to fill effectively because any activity arranged to fill them needs to be shelved immediately, and maybe postponed indefinitely, if work does come in.

It is not uncommon for EDT shifts to be quiet for some time until one or two calls disrupt the calm entirely and subsequently occupy the workers completely for several hours. Like all emergency services EDT workers are paid primarily for their availability. Fire fighters may not be called out for days or weeks on end but the public wants them to be ready and able to respond if needed, whenever this may be. Before going home the 'overnight' worker will fax, telephone or e-mail details of any work undertaken by EDT to the relevant daytime team. They may also make an accompanying telephone call if appropriate. In addition to working the two evening shifts described every night of the year, EDTs will also cover daytime shifts over weekends and bank holiday periods. One characteristic of working in an EDT is the mercurial nature of the work to be done. Workers can think they are dealing with one issue, only to find, a few minutes later, that it has changed into something else. A necessary skill to cultivate is that of learning how to expect the unexpected!

Constantly changing challenges

An extreme example of how rapidly things can change occurred one evening when the EDT worker on duty received a call from an ambulance crew on their way to a woman believed to have died in her garage. She had attached a hosepipe to the exhaust pipe of her car and was thought to have gassed herself. The woman had three children who had not been told of what had happened and their father was unavailable. The worker needed to think through how they were going to involve the children and respond to their needs for both accommodation and emotional support. A few minutes later the ambulance crew telephoned again, this time to report that the woman was not dead, as first thought, but was very drowsy and confused. Her husband, the children's father, was thought to be on his way. During the next half an hour the EDT worker was kept up to date as the drama unfolded and, in the end, was not required to do anything apart from pass the information on to the daytime team. While the calls were coming through from the ambulance crew other requests for involvement in other different child protection crises were made along with a request for an appropriate adult for a young person who had shot at a teacher with an air rifle.

Referrals such as these can 'hit' EDT workers arriving for duty almost before they have had time to take their coat off. The antagonistic feeling of pressing urgency to act in some crucial way alternating with a realisation that nothing is required after all, is a frequent feature of EDT work.

One of the most helpful lessons that experienced workers learn and constantly relearn is that given time, things often change. A particularly helpful piece of advice given some years ago by a colleague was, 'Whenever you have a particularly serious crisis the first thing you should do is to make a hot drink and hold it in your hands'. When a combination of crises seems particularly overwhelming then taking a step back to slow down, establish some distance, get warm, and think is often a useful first step.

On another occasion the police telephoned EDT at 2.00 a.m. to say they had entered a house to find nine young children in bed with no responsible adult looking after them so could they please be accommodated? This is a heart-sink moment for an EDT worker who counts themselves fortunate if they have one or two places to accommodate children, let alone nine. A few minutes later, having made a hot drink and sat there, alone in the quiet, holding it in their hands, wondering what to do, the worker was extremely relieved to hear back from the police that no accommodation was necessary after all. They had discovered that one of the nine people in the house was an adult. In the darkness and the excitement of the crisis the police had not realised this at first – thus events changed from impossible-looking problem to instant solution in fifteen minutes!

In a different and tragic situation a mother was suspected of killing one of her six children, leaving the remaining five needing to be looked after. After hours of telephoning around only two foster parents could be found, miles away from each other, able to take only three children between them. Deliberations about what could be tried next were interrupted by the sudden and unexpected appearance of the children's grandmother who took all of the children away with her with the agreement of their mother.

Service users can also change considerably in mood, coping skills and attitude within a very short time. A 15-year-old's mother telephoned to say that he had completely exhausted her patience. She hated him, she loathed him, she despised him and never wanted to see him again. If he came back to her house she would kill him. She spent some time articulating this with the force and fury of 'justified' wrath which characterises much communication from despairing parents of wayward adolescents. The power of her invective was considerable. She said the reason for her call was so that if the police picked him up and contacted EDT they would be in no doubt that he was their responsibility. She didn't care *what* happened to him, provided she was not troubled any further about his future. An hour or so later the police did pick him up and contacted the team. Knowing that, despite what she had said, his mother retained parental responsibility for him under The Children Act 1989 she was telephoned, with some trepidation, fearing the response she may make. Speaking to her the second time was like speaking to a different person. She was polite, reasonable, measured and concerned about him. Of course she would contact the police about him, of course she would have him back . . . yes she knew she was angry when she spoke about him earlier but she had calmed down now and she loved him really, he was a *good* boy, really . . . It is remarkable to witness how quickly and how fundamentally people can change what they say and how they act. Though some of these changes may be for the better, this capacity in human beings helps to provide some insight into the states of mind in which some people may abuse others and feel justified, even vindicated, while doing so. Perhaps as soon as only a few minutes after the abuse they may be regretting what they have said or done but at the moment, for that moment, they believed what they were doing was nothing more than they were entitled to do.

In drama therapy literature (Johnstone, 1993; Ives, 1997) these profound changes are described as changes in the different roles performed by the same person. Berne (1975) claims that, in particular, changes between the roles of victim, persecutor and rescuer can take place extremely quickly. Elsewhere Briere (1992), Sinason (1994) and Garland (1998) have claimed that a dissociative process is at work whereby one part of the person is split off from the rest of them. This is illustrated by phrases such as 'I don't know what came over me', 'I'm in two minds about that' and 'I was beside myself with rage'. A mother of a 15-year-old young woman at a police station talked in these terms. She had taken her daughter to the station and 'turned herself in' at 1.00 a.m. one morning having suddenly found herself banging her daughter's head repeatedly on the kitchen wall. She said that she had suddenly 'snapped' out of the state in which she was committing this act of violence to find herself amazed and shocked that she could treat her daughter in such a way. The last thing she remembered before 'snapping' out of the state was arguing with her daughter and her daughter retorting, 'Well, *you* created me!' The woman felt like Dr Frankenstein twice – firstly, for giving birth to her daughter who became a monster that turned on her and secondly for producing the hateful feelings that made her want to assault her creation. Working at EDT can provide a salutary reminder of the extremes of thought and behaviour of which human beings are capable.

In another example the mother of a young woman telephoned EDT just before midnight insisting that her daughter was terrible, awful; she deserved no sympathy. She had been having sex with boyfriends, missing school, drinking alcohol, taking drugs, stealing and generally putting herself in danger. Her mother had sought help from daytime social services teams but had become increasingly frustrated with their responses. She felt that they wanted to blame her rather than understand her. She explained, 'They keep saying that it's my husband and I who are the problem but it's not – it's her'. Her tone in talking of this was that of one outraged and hurting adult to another, sympathetic adult who would see things the way she did and agree with her. She expected little response and seemed to have called to convey her view at length and have this heard and not disputed. The mother called back an hour and a half later talking in a very different tone of voice – vulnerable, defeated, anxious, concerned. Her daughter had still not returned home. She was not answering her mobile telephone. Her mother was worried about her now, where was she, who was she with, was she ok? She was only fifteen after all . . . The mother said she was going to report her missing to the police. Again, it was like talking to a different person entirely. Within a short space of time her tone had changed from sounding vindicated, justified, haughty and condemning to seeming more like a vulnerable little girl herself, frightened in the dark, in need of comfort and reassurance.

This chapter concludes with some thoughts about how to optimise good practice in working relationships between EDTs, daytime teams and partner agencies.

Recommendations for good practice in working relationships between daytime teams, partner agencies and EDTs

- EDTs prefer referrals to be brief, typed and faxed or e-mailed with a clear indication of the desired response/course of action to be taken.
- It is sometimes helpful for this typed information to be accompanied by a brief telephone call.
- In addition to the referral and preferred plan it is helpful to provide the telephone number of someone who can assist in case of an unexpected turn of events.
- Delegated powers should be clearly specified and identified. Senior managers distinguish between when they want to be contacted and when they are willing for EDT to make decisions in their absence and on their behalf.
- EDTs should provide a typed, clear and concise account of the development of any situation they deal with. This should be faxed or e-mailed back to the referrer with an accompanying telephone call if necessary.
- The account should include a risk assessment, where appropriate, explaining how and why decisions were arrived at and why different decisions were not made.
- Outcomes of EDT involvement should be clear as should the needs for any ongoing or follow-up work by daytime staff.
- Ideally there will be some form of regular, ongoing liaison between EDT and daytime teams/partner agencies whereby individual case studies and general principles can be shared, discussed and learnt from away from the heat of a crisis.

Practice

CHAPTER 2

Child care and child protection work

This chapter outlines the roles and responsibilities of EDTs when working with children and young people. A child is defined here as being under 18 years of age as in The Children Act 1989. Consideration is first given to the needs of babies and younger children and then to adolescents. An analysis of the relevance for EDTs of *The framework for the assessment of children in need and their families* (Department of Health, 2000) follows and the impact upon workers of dealing with child care and child protection issues is highlighted. The chapter ends with some recommendations for good practice.

Babies and young children

An EDT may have to begin to consider a baby's needs and safety even before it is born. There have been several instances where women about to give birth in hospital have been referred to EDT because their, as yet, unborn baby is already on the child protection register and/or thought to be at risk. In such cases an EDT may be asked to work with the hospital to ensure that the mother and baby remain on the ward together until the next working day when appropriate arrangements can be made with and by the daytime team. It may be that police protection (section 47 of The Children Act 1989) is thought necessary in which case the EDT and the police need to be working in partnership and discussing the issues together. In general EDTs work closely with the police and their power of police protection. This power gives the police the authority to secure the safety of a child, if need be against the wishes of those with parental responsibility and without their knowledge. The power lasts for up to 72 hours. Even when EDTs are covering a four-day stretch because a two-day bank holiday precedes or follows a weekend the three-day duration of police protection usually suffices thereby making the consideration of an Emergency Protection Order (EPO) unnecessary. In any event EPOs are best left to the daytime teams who will have both more knowledge of the case and access to the relevant specialist legal advice.

EDTs may also become involved in cases of suspected Munchausen Syndrome by Proxy (MSP) (Levin and Sheridan, 1995). In this strange and often perplexing illness (also known as factitious illness) caretakers of (usually) young children – often their mothers – manufacture apparent symptoms of illness in their child because they gain some vicarious satisfaction from the medical attention, and resultant interventions and treatment. In extreme cases children can die – either as a result of what the mother does to them in order to induce the symptoms of illness or as a side effect of medical interventions that were not necessary in the first place. Mothers systematically feeding high doses of salt to their child or mixing their own menstrual blood in their child's urine sample and presenting it to a doctor as being the child's are examples of this syndrome. MSP can be notoriously difficult to recognise for two principal reasons: first, people don't want to believe that a mother could want to fabricate serious illness in her child (see the discussion of 'the rule of optimism' in Chapter 6) and, secondly, the mothers are often very convincing and highly skilled at concealing what they are doing. An EDT was once called on a Saturday to respond to a case of MSP where a mother was shown to be surreptitiously disconnecting life-saving equipment from her young child by a hospital security camera. The legal and ethical issues of dealing with MSP are complex and multi-faceted. As in all child protection work, sound and effective partnership working is essential between social workers, health workers and police officers (see Chapter 8).

On other occasions EDTs will deal with carers who, although not going so far as to create apparent illnesses in their children as in MSP, will still use their children as an indirect way of communicating their own extreme distress. Sometimes mothers seem unable to distinguish between their own identity and needs, and those of their child. An extreme example of this is the mother cited in Kempe and Kempe (1978) who said that her child could not possibly want food since *she* was not hungry! When mothers are mentally ill or abuse drugs and alcohol such difficulties are compounded.

One mother, with a history of heavy use of non-prescribed drugs and a diagnosed personality disorder called an EDT at 4 a.m. Without introducing herself she told the worker on duty to come and remove her young child immediately. The worker, on duty alone, recognised her as being a regular caller and asked for a few moments to update themselves on recent developments and plans. The mother replied, 'No, that's it. You've had your chance – it's your fault you haven't taken it' and hung up. The worker called her back but she did not answer the telephone. She lived some 30 miles away from the EDT base. Following an anxious time of reflection the worker followed a course of action, well rehearsed by EDTs in such instances, and contacted the local police service. The duty officer answering the call said, 'I'm so pleased to have heard from you as a woman has 'phoned us saying, "I'm sat here in front of a baby that I hate and I don't know what I'm going to do to it". We have not been able to trace the call and don't recognise her, and we think the child may be at serious risk'. As the EDT worker was able to provide the address the police visited quickly. They found the door of the mother's flat open and mother and child were apparently peacefully asleep.

It is hard to know why calls such as these are made to EDTs. On the one hand it seems that there is a malicious desire to provoke anxiety and uncertainty in professionals who are paid to keep others safe and well. On the other, such callers often seem chaotic and disorganised to the extent that they are unable to appreciate the likely repercussions of their communications. These calls may represent a hurt and angry cry to parent-substitute authority figures – a demand to be noticed. Whatever the explanation, calls like this one cause intense concern for those receiving them. It is therefore helpful for all professionals concerned to assess these situations and their inherent risks together and thereby pool knowledge, skills and ultimately, responsibility, when trying to decide how best to respond.

N, the mother of a two year-old child, S, had a history of sexual abuse and mental health problems and called the EDT one Sunday night at 6.30 p.m. She was sobbing and distraught on the telephone to the extent that she was barely comprehensible. She had been to a psychiatric day hospital earlier in the day and returned from this with her child to stay at the house of another service user. She said she had been experiencing horrific flashbacks about her abuse in the form of hallucinations. She said she was 'evil' and could not be a good mother to her child and that he would be better off without her. She did not want to speak to the duty covering doctor as she anticipated they would only increase her medication and she was sick and tired of being over-medicated by people who did not know her. She asked to go into the local psychiatric ward but there were no beds available. After talking for some time she sounded more composed and said she would stay with her friend until the morning when she could access daytime workers and services. The EDT worker thought she was sufficiently rational to make this decision safely and so agreed with it. Half an hour later she called back to thank the worker for listening and supporting her.

At 11 p.m. she called again, having reversed the charges from a call box. She began, breathing heavily, 'I've done something awful to S'. This kind of statement often blurted out by service users as an introduction to a communication is a 'heart-sink' moment for the EDT worker hearing it. A multitude of thoughts rush through the mind about all manner of awful possibilities as the worker attempts to brace themselves for they know not what . . . It emerged that she had told her young son that he would be better off without her, that 'another mummy and daddy would be better for him' and rushed out of the house leaving him with her friend. The worker could hear traffic from the road passing by with loud 'swishing' noises as she spoke on the telephone and wondered if she was considering throwing herself in front of it.

A constantly recurring dilemma for EDT workers involves deciding whether a situation can be held (contained) or whether some form of action needs to be taken. Having spoken to N earlier the worker could have shared the responsibility of the decision by contacting the on-call doctor and asking them to visit or contact her despite her saying that she did not want this. A recognised tension in crisis intervention generally and mental health work in particular (see Chapter 3) is that service users' views need to be taken into account but must sometimes be over-ridden if people are thought not to be able to make decisions that are in their best interests. Sometimes EDT workers may look back on an intervention and think they ought not to have made it. On other occasions, as in this case, the concern may be that they should have acted but did not. There is a fine line between trying to help service users access their strengths and undermining this process by calling in extra help when it is not needed and recognising that, at times, those strengths may not be there to access. Risk assessments might be of some help at these times, and should be completed but, even the best informed, most carefully thought through risk assessment is prone to error (see Chapter 6).

The worker thought that the best chance of helping N was to appeal to her love for S and so stressed how much S needed her and would want to see her again even though she had hurt him. N couldn't return to her own house even if she wanted to as she had left her keys at her friend's house. She said she just needed to walk. Provided she could do this safely, the worker thought this might be a good idea since a combination of the time and space away from S and her friend, the exercise, and cold night air might exercise a calming influence on her. The worker said he would speak with N's friend to check how they saw things and call N back on her mobile 'phone. N's friend was reasonable and understanding saying that she appreciated N was having a difficult time but did not think she should have spoken to S as she had done. N's friend was willing to have N back, however, and said she would not be cross with her when she returned. The friend then said, 'I hope she doesn't do anything rash' and this statement echoed the worker's earlier passing thought that N might throw herself in front of the traffic. Once again the dilemma between wanting to encourage people's self-determination and recognising that they sometimes need protection from themselves presented itself. The worker knew that there was the option of contacting the police but also believed that N would feel undermined by that. On balance, the friend didn't think that N would 'do anything rash' but also 'didn't want to be the one to make that decision'. The worker tended to agree with that assessment but still felt uncomfortable because he had earlier assessed N to be less troubled than she turned out to be.

The worker contacted N and told her what her friend had said. Recognising that N would need time to compose herself the worker asked that she should return to her friend's by midnight and telephone to confirm that she had done so. An anxious wait followed but N did call back at 11.45 p.m. saying that she was now back with her friend and S. She sounded contrite and subdued. She agreed to try to get through the night the best she could (she had not slept through the night for a long time). Having checked that the arrangement was agreeable to N's friend the worker said he would call at 8 a.m. to check on how things were. During that subsequent call it appeared that the situation had held and was calm. N agreed to contact her daytime workers and a report was faxed through to them by the EDT worker. Fortunately, this crisis was resolved safely.

On other occasions EDTs may be dealing with more tragic outcomes such as one where a mother had set fire to her house and thus killed her sleeping daughter inside, and another where a mother had fallen asleep on her young infant and suffocated her. These brief but intense engagements with the awful consequences of, often unintended, actions can stay with EDT workers for a long time afterwards and might affect their decision making in subsequent similar situations. This has implications for the support and supervision that is made available to them (see Chapter 7).

EDTs will get called to situations of domestic violence, often in the early hours of the morning. A mother may have been admitted to hospital having been assaulted by a man who has then disappeared, leaving young children in need of care. The police will often be the first to attend such an incident and will contact EDT to discuss child care arrangements. Babies and young children might be left in houses, asleep and alone, blissfully unaware that there is no adult in the house to care for them. If the nearest foster placement is several miles away, as is often the case in the larger counties, it can be a mystifying and disturbing experience for a young child to be suddenly removed from a familiar environment by complete strangers and driven miles in the dark then to be handed over to different strangers and left with them. Whenever possible it is therefore desirable that someone sits with the child throughout the journey to offer such comfort and explanation as is possible.

Adolescents

Adolescence has been described as a time of 'storm and stress' in the life cycle when problems of identity loom large, disputes with authority are frequent and rebellion, deviance and delinquency commonplace (Erikson, 1968; Meyerson, 1975). Other commentators claim that the anti-social aspects of adolescence have been overstated and that many families' experiences of adolescence are bearable, even interesting and enjoyable (Rutter and Rutter, 1993; Coleman and Hendry, 1999). EDTs however, will usually become involved with adolescents and their families when things are not going well and when one or more people are making this known.

J, aged 14, was 'thrown out' by his mother one New Year's eve. He had been suspended from school and rejected by his peers. He was causing arguments with his siblings and was being disobedient to his mother who was struggling to bring up three children on her own. He used sexually inappropriate and offensive language to her and, influenced by gangsta-rap music, was insulting and derogatory towards her. Their disagreements culminated with him kicking the back door in and her throwing him out into the cold and rain, without a coat. He called EDT, early in the evening, reversing the charges from a call box near where he lived. One of the problems faced by EDTs in circumstances such as these is the lack of resources where young people can go to wait while situations are discussed and alternatives negotiated. The EDT worker discussed J's circumstances with the police who picked him up and took him to the police station as a place of safety while options were investigated. J was not pleased about this course of action but recognised that he had no choice.

In cases like J's EDTs will first investigate whether family or friends can help. In this case they couldn't and New Year's eve was not a good time to find people available to discuss the predicament of a child in need and at risk of significant harm under the terms of The Children Act 1989. Social workers have to work with the tension of knowing their legal obligations to young people in need but with the fact that they have few (and sometimes no) resources. They also know that legally, parents have 'parental responsibility' for their children whatever their current feelings may be. While every attempt is made to encourage and help those with parental responsibility to accept and fulfil their obligations there are still times when people will absolutely refuse to make arrangements for the appropriate care of their children. On such occasions those in the caring professions have no choice but to step into this role. The social worker visited J's mother to discuss the situation with her. On this occasion it was sufficiently safe for one worker to visit her alone. On other occasions it may be thought necessary for two workers to visit and this presents difficulties for some EDTs who are typically minimally staffed (see Chapter 1) and may not have two staff available to visit together at a particular time. J's mother was adamant that she would not change her mind and that she knew of no other people who could take him. In any event, she didn't care. It was 'over to us' now and not her problem any longer.

A place was found for J in a local children's home where he stayed for several days before being returned home with support from an adolescent outreach team. Sometimes there are no places for young people in or outside of the county or borough covered by an EDT. In recent years the trend has been to close down children's homes and to use the money to fund the community-based outreach teams who work with families to keep young people at home. This situation has arisen partly because it is recognised that children's homes may have disadvantages for young people (Garratt, 1999) but there is still a need for adequate resources to be available in cases of absolute necessity. Williams (1997) has shown that parents and children having difficulties with one another will often value the opportunity to talk about their problems and be listened to carefully. Nevertheless she also demonstrates that there are still times when listening is not enough and other resources are needed. This can often present a dilemma for the EDT worker who may believe the provision of a resource to be necessary and yet have none to offer. One EDT worker was discussing such a case with a police inspector who was getting increasingly annoyed about what he saw to be 'social services' failure to meet their clear responsibility under The Children Act 1989. The worker said she understood and agreed with his argument. He retorted, 'I don't want your *understanding*, I want you to *do* something about it'.

Sometimes a helpful friend or helpful friends' helpful parents will become involved with young people's problems. The young person may present as reasonable, unfortunate and misunderstood to friends and their parents who consequently want to help out. Such people may offer accommodation to the young person. This may resolve an immediate dilemma about where the young person stays that night but might simultaneously trigger longer-term difficulties and resentments with the young person's parents, particularly if they live just around the corner! In one case the parents' anger and sadness that their adolescent daughter no longer wanted to stay with them was compounded by their belief that she was misrepresenting them to the neighbours and 'rubbing their noses in it' by giving the impression that her friends' parents possessed the qualities which they lacked.

Another situation increasingly being encountered by those working with adolescents is that of self-harm and suicide. Jamison (2000: 21, 48, 202) draws attention to the recently escalating figures for suicide and self-harm in the adolescent population in the United States:

> *Suicide in the young, which has at least tripled over the past forty-five years, is, without argument, one of our most serious public health problems. Suicide is the third leading cause of death in young people in the United States and the second for college students . . . In the United States between 1980 and 1992 the rate of suicide in children aged ten to fourteen increased by 120 per cent. In 1995, more teenagers and young adults died from suicide than died from cancer, heart disease, AIDS, pneumonia, influenza, birth defects and stroke combined . . . puberty . . . coincides with the first significant rise in the rate of suicide.*

Aldridge (1998) identifies this concern as being relevant also to the United Kingdom. It is likely that the true extent of adolescent suicide is under-represented. Coroners may be reluctant to decide upon a suicide verdict when an adolescent has died as this may distress family members (Hawton, 1986; Aldridge, 1998). Despite this, Hawton (1986) argues that evidence of suicidal behaviour can be found in children under five and Bagley and Ramsey (1997) document incidents of suicide by ten and 12-year-olds. The current concern about rising suicide rates in the United Kingdom has prompted the government's introduction of a *Suicide Prevention Strategy* (Department of Health, 2002) – see Chapter 3.

At 2 a.m. an EDT worker heard from a foster parent that a 15-year-old she had been looking after for two years without incident had taken an overdose, 'completely out of the blue'. It emerged that the young person had been bullied at school, rejected by her peer group, fallen out with her boyfriend, impulsively decided that she wanted to die and so had taken the tablets. The foster mother had found her and taken her to the accident and emergency department of the local hospital. After consultation between the foster parent, doctors and social worker it was decided that it was sufficiently safe for the young person to return to the care of the foster parent with subsequent outpatient support also arranged. The foster parent was quite taken aback by the young woman's behaviour as she had not 'seen it coming' at all.

One of the reasons identified by Bagley and Ramsey (1997) for the current high rates of suicidal behaviour by young people is their perception of suicide as a reasonable and feasible option far more readily than the previous generation. People in the previous generation are more likely to see themselves as 'tightening their belts' in adversity and 'clinging on' when times get hard. Members of the current generation, by contrast, are more likely to think it quite reasonable to kill themselves if things are not going well. EDT workers need to be mindful of the vulnerability of young people to suicidal thoughts and feelings and the possibility that they may act on these feelings. This can make the paucity of available resources referred to earlier difficult to justify and work with (or, more accurately, work without).

One way in which the importance of the wider picture including community and neighbourhood resources is acknowledged is by way of *The Framework for the Assessment of Children in Need and their Families* (Department of Health, 2000).

The framework for the assessment of children in need and their families

The *Framework* is drawn in the form of a triangle. The child is placed inside the triangle at its centre indicating the fact that the child is meant to remain as the centre and focus of concern. Along one side of the triangle are listed seven of the *child's developmental needs*, namely, the needs for health, education, emotional and behavioural development, identity, family and social relationships, social presentation and self-care skills. Another side of the triangle concerns *parenting capacity* which is defined as including the provision of basic care, emotional warmth, age-appropriate stimulation, guidance and boundaries, and stability within the context of ensuring safety. The third side of the triangle relates to *family and environmental factors* that comprise family history, functioning and social integration, the wider family, housing, employment, income and other community resources. The underlying organising idea behind the *Framework* is that children can be holistically assessed only if each of the three sides of the triangle, with their constituent sub-divisions are taken into consideration.

While it may be helpful for EDT workers to have family and environmental factors acknowledged as being important in the lives of children and young people, they are not going to be able to create resources while working. The police inspector, quoted above, who said he wanted the EDT worker to *do* something, did not, presumably, expect her to be able to create a resource there and then, but his frustration was understandable given that so few resources are available for problems that are eminently foreseeable. Working with the third side of the triangle that relates to family and environmental factors entails what Jack (2000: 704, 713) describes as the ecological approach:

> . . . *insufficient attention continues to be given, with social work policies and practices, to the structural and environmental factors that are at the root of most of the problems experienced by families . . . The ecological approach to social work with children and families is not something which can merely be added to the social worker's 'tool kit' of skills and techniques, to be used selectively, as and when appropriate. Rather, it should be thought of as the tool kit itself, out of which the various methods of assessment and intervention can be selected.*

This view echoes Thompson's (1991) contention that, in order to be effective, crisis social work needs to recognise structural social divisions, including class, race and gender. The 'community workers' employed by social services departments some years ago worked with wider systems and networks rather than within one-to-one casework relationships and provide an example of an attempt to work in this more general structural context. In reality, however, adopting an 'ecological approach' is easier theorised and written about than implemented. Many social work teams are under-staffed and cannot recruit and retain sufficient workers:

> *The problems being experienced by most councils and other social care employers in the recruitment and retention of staff is hindering the modernisation process and the achievement of national targets for social care services ... Birmingham reports a current overall vacancy rate of 26 per cent; some London Boroughs have reported vacancy rates for qualified social workers of up to 40 per cent.*

(Department of Health, 2001: 59)

Social workers who are in post are rarely able to think about and engage with the kind of work with wider systems integral to the ecological approach. As practitioners struggle to respond to increasing demands and diminishing resources the cases nearest crisis are (understandably) given priority while any thoughts about prevention recede into the distance. The government has attempted to recognise and address some of these difficulties, for example, by the introduction of *Sure Start* initiatives with families living in the most socially deprived areas. There are rare examples of successful work with and within wider communities such as the 'social action psychotherapy' described by Holland (1995) but generally an ecological approach to children and families in need is more of a hope than a reality at present. One way of attempting to promote an ecological approach is to work with voluntary and community groups. EDTs are often contacted by other agencies such as the *National Society for the Prevention of Cruelty to Children* or *Childline* to pass on concerns about danger, abuse or unhappiness. Sometimes the detail from these calls can be passed on for the attention of daytime teams the next working day but sometimes a more immediate response is necessary.

Other work undertaken with adolescents includes attendance at police stations, to accompany those under 18 years old, in the role of *appropriate adult* for interviews conducted under The Police and Criminal Evidence Act 1984 (Littlechild, 1996). Some EDT members may attend such interviews themselves on occasions, sometimes there may be various sessional worker or voluntary schemes in place. Who attends, and when, is usually determined by local policy, the seriousness and timing of the alleged offence, whether the young person is in the care of the local authority and the availability (or lack) of suitable other people. EDTs often become involved in discussions about who can and should return children who have left their original area of residence to come to light in other areas of the country, or even abroad. Low staffing levels and health and safety considerations (see Chapter 6) combine to make it highly unlikely that EDT workers themselves will retrieve such children. Residential units and foster carers are also unlikely to be willing or able to assist. Often this means that the police are left 'holding on' to young people until suitable arrangements can be made, sometimes by way of expensive 'escorting' agencies. There is growing awareness and concern about the vulnerability of young runaways –

currently estimated as 77,000 per annum in the United Kingdom, including nearly 20,000 who are aged under 11 (Social Exclusion Unit, 2002). EDTs and the police are frequently in contact with these young people but lack of staff, little time and competing other priorities combine to result in little meaningful work being attempted with them.

Giving support to foster carers is another task of EDTs and this may range from providing a 'listening ear' when things are difficult to making alternative arrangements in cases of placement breakdown. EDT workers cannot always be available when foster carers may want to talk to them and this has led to schemes being established in some areas where a dedicated rota of workers are available specifically to provide support to foster carers when they need it.

Throughout all of the situations outlined above there is the need for EDTs to be mindful of the influence of parental mental illness, problem alcohol and drug use, and domestic violence upon the capacity and ability of parent figures to act safely and appropriately (Cleaver et al., 1999). Dealing with these variables of the human condition, often in intense and concentrated forms, has an impact on EDT workers. Even the most experienced, skilful, detached and defended worker will, at times, find themselves reacting to a situation much more 'personally' than they would choose (see Chapter 7).

The impact of working with children on EDT workers

Childhood and old age are the times in the life cycle for most people when they are at their most vulnerable and EDTs are frequently dealing with people's extreme vulnerabilities. Others may perceive EDT workers as having developed a hard 'macho' front: 'We can cope with anything (and often do!)'. It may be that this image conceals a fear of vulnerability because EDT workers are particularly aware of the fragility of human beings and the vagaries of chance that repeatedly affect them. Because they cover at least three-quarters of the working week the law of averages predicts that EDT workers will often be on duty to experience the first full impact of tragedies resulting from a brief loss of attention or ill-advised action. For example, the mentally ill daughter who murdered both of her parents and came out of a trance to realise what she had done. Calls conveying such information come unannounced, 'out of the blue' and are likely to be received by a worker, sitting alone in an office in hours of darkness. The initially-remembered impact and consequent aftermath of these kind of calls can stay with workers for years to come. Provision of effective and timely support and supervision for staff should be a major management concern and priority (see Chapter 7).

Like every adult, all EDT workers were once children themselves. Because of this certain events they deal with may resonate with their own family experience and early emotions and therefore influence their response. As Covey (1992: 245) writes, we, 'listen autobiographically' – i.e. within the framework and value base of our own history and upbringing – and evaluate, probe, advise or interpret accordingly. Examples of 'autobiographical listening' have been recalled by female EDT workers when pregnant and shortly after giving birth. One experienced female EDT worker said that she had only been assaulted twice in twenty years of EDT work. Both times were when she was pregnant. Reflecting on this, she thought that, when in the presence of a potentially violent service user, she would have been particularly mindful of her unborn baby. Because she was carrying the baby, and therefore felt responsible for another life as well as her own, she thought she may have feared more (or feared differently) than she would have done were she not pregnant. She thought the service users in question could have 'picked up' on this 'different' and therefore less-processed-than-usual fear of hers, subsequently felt worried themselves, and therefore attacked her. Another female worker who had recently given birth to her first child described visiting a new-born baby of heroin-addicted parents. There were considerable concerns for the baby and the parents' ability to care for it properly. The accommodation was squalid, there had been violence between the parents and the baby's well being seemed in jeopardy. The worker described how, while looking at this sad situation and sickly looking baby, she found herself repeatedly thinking of her own new child and the hope she felt for him. This enabled her to be hopeful for the baby of the service users she was visiting.

Sometimes EDT workers who are also parents will be dealing with situations uncomfortably 'close to home'. One worker left home for a shift having walked away from a particularly heated row with his adolescent son. As soon as he arrived at work he took a call from a parent embroiled in a row with her adolescent that had much in common with the argument he had just left. The service user's argument had developed beyond his own, criminal damage had been caused and the police became involved. While dealing with the call the worker found it hard to differentiate which of his thoughts and feelings belonged to his own home situation and which to that of the service user. Having dealt with the work situation he telephoned home to check his son was OK and apologise to him.

EDT work provides a frequent reminder of how great destruction can erupt from small beginnings such as a dispute about tidying a bedroom or playing music loudly. Such arguments can culminate in children smashing possessions and property, family members assaulting one another and parents refusing to let children stay at home.

EDT workers may have lost children of their own, and feelings about these losses might become activated and recalled when service users call to mourn their losses. One EDT worker 'snapped' at a caller in the early hours of the morning when he was justifying why he had let his young child down and seeking her support for his action. Having dealt with the child previously and identified with the distress caused by his father's neglect she thought the father grossly irresponsible and could not stop herself from telling him so. The father subsequently complained and, arguably, had a case. On the other hand, EDT social workers are 'only human' and it is extremely hard to remain totally detached and 'professional' when responding to all highly emotive situations, particularly those which 'ring bells' within our own life experience. Again, this indicates the need for skilled, sensitive, and appropriate supervision and support for EDT workers, despite their considerable self-awareness, experience, resilience and autonomy (see Chapter 7).

Recommendations for good practice in child care and child protection work

- Workers should recognise that adults, knowingly or unknowingly, may use the children they care for to draw attention to their own difficulties and conflicts.

- The impact of parental mental illness, problem alcohol and drug use, and domestic violence on children's development, well-being and safety should be acknowledged and responded to where necessary.

- The needs of those who deliberately harm themselves and run away from problematic situations should be responded to thoughtfully and appropriately.

- The child's developmental needs, parent's capacity to parent properly, and wider 'ecological' factors should be considered in assessments.

- Services and voluntary agencies out of hours should have partnership agreements and effective joint-working protocols.

- The potential impact of the work on workers undertaking it should be recognised and appropriate support mechanisms are provided and available.

- Resources and staffing levels are such that the above can be more reality than rhetoric.

CHAPTER 3

Mental health work

This chapter focuses on the needs of service users with mental health problems who refer themselves to EDTs. It contrasts this group with those who are typically referred by others for assessment under The Mental Health Act (MHA) 1983. The pros and cons of asking EDTs to make check calls on behalf of daytime teams are considered. Following a brief resume of the principles integral to working with the MHA, the 'other-referred' group is considered under three main age categories; children, adults and older people since each of these groups has its own specific needs and is normally the responsibility of different specialist psychiatrists. The chapter concludes with recommendations for good practice in mental health work. Assessing and managing risks of those who may represent a danger to themselves or others is integral to mental health work and these aspects of the work are addressed in Chapter 6.

Self-referrers

These are a small but well-defined group of people with mental health problems who choose to call EDTs frequently. They may not be able to sleep, they may find themselves obsessively ruminating on their difficulties or they may just want to talk and decide that staff on duty at EDT are who they want to talk to. Some may be people with a history of self-harm who have learnt that they are less likely to harm themselves if they talk about how they feel with someone else. Sometimes callers prefer to talk to particular workers whom they have come to favour so they put the telephone down if one of those workers does not answer the call. Sometimes their intention seems to be to abuse and hurt the EDT worker and derogatory, threatening or explicitly sexual insults may be conveyed or left as ansaphone messages.

EDTs may try to educate callers and re-direct them to other services such as The Samaritans and Saneline (thought to be more appropriate for people who essentially want to talk and have others listen to them). Nevertheless callers are often clear about why they have contacted EDT rather than one of the other agencies. When one service user was asked why she had contacted EDT rather than The Samaritans since it seemed she did not have an emergency in the EDT sense of the word and primarily wanted to 'just talk', she replied that Samaritans, 'never say anything – they just listen'. In this respect she was right as The Samaritans are trained to provide a listening response to callers and will not usually offer advice, suggestions or guidance. A house-bound service user who was a constant caller to EDT reasoned that as she didn't smoke, drink or gamble her calls to EDT were a little luxury that she could allow herself.

EDT workers are not always available at the other end of the telephone as they may be out on visits. When they do answer calls, they may attempt to encourage callers to contact them about only 'core business', but they cannot actually prevent people from calling. In this sense the service users determine the timing, frequency and (often) duration of calls thereby enabling them to control essential aspects of the communication process. One repeat caller who telephoned frequently about relatively trivial-seeming matters was told firmly by his rehabilitation officer that he should contact EDT only in cases of genuine emergency. His response was to telephone just as frequently as before but to preface each call with the words, 'This is a genuine emergency . . .' Sometimes attempts are made to limit service users to certain times, frequency and duration of contact with services in the day. EDTs may attempt to impose similar restrictions but enforcing them is often problematic and ultimately impossible.

The difficulty in responding to these calls is that one never knows when an apparently trivial situation is in fact a genuine emergency. Workers may get lulled into a false sense of security when responding to repeat callers and become over-familiar with hearing what sounds like the same story repeated many times. Just because someone has not acted previously on constant threats to harm themselves or others does not mean that they will not do so. A particular difficulty here is to avoid the equal and opposite dangers of over, and under, reaction. Thoughtful risk assessment may be helpful (see Chapter 6) but for some people even the most thorough risk assessment will fail to predict certain outcomes. Human nature is never one hundred per cent predictable but having protocols and procedures discussed and agreed with daytime workers and partner agencies (in particular the police and ambulance services) will help to promote confidence and clarity for EDT workers needing to respond in a crisis.

Check calls

A daytime worker may anticipate difficulties for a service user over a particular weekend and ask EDT to make a 'check call' (or, more rarely, visit) to inquire as to how the service user is getting on. Whilst such check calls have been shown to be appreciated by people with a history of self-harm (Vaughan, 1995), it is questionable whether EDTs are the best people to make them. Because EDTs have to be ready to respond to emergencies they cannot, by definition, guarantee to attend to any planned work. The best they can offer is to say that they will make the call if time and other priorities allow but this may not be adequate if the service user is thought to need a call, particularly at a certain time. Moreover, EDTs have sometimes made check calls and later regretted it. The service user may have apparently been getting on quite well until the call served as an unpleasant and unwanted reminder of their problems. The service user therefore resents the intrusion and the worker may be left with the feeling that they have stirred things up and done more harm than good. There are currently plans to include evening hours coverage by Community Mental Health Teams. This initiative, together with the creation of home treatment and assertive outreach/rapid response crisis teams, means that any supportive/checking function can in future be carried out by those who are more likely to have prior knowledge and experience of working with the person concerned.

It is only rarely the case that people referring themselves will need assessment under the MHA because by instigating communication they have recognised their need and brought this to the attention of services. The motivation of such people and their willingness to co-operate can be variable however. They may identify a significant, perhaps urgent problem but then state a refusal to co-operate further. They may be ambivalent and inconsistent so that even if they do agree to co-operate this agreement does not always indicate the presence of the mental capacity necessary for fully informed consent. A check call made by EDT or a check visit from another support worker may reveal situations in need of further assessment; EDT may be called by a family member or another agency to alert them to a person struggling with their mental health. In all such cases an assessment under the MHA will need to be considered.

Principles of Mental Health Act Assessments

Most full time EDT workers are approved social workers (ASWs) under the terms of the MHA 1983 or are undertaking training to become approved. For this role they will complete a post-qualifying training course (currently of approximately sixty days duration) which authorises them to make applications for compulsory detention of patients under the Act. Whilst a 'nearest relative' (defined in MHA section 26) can and sometimes does make an application for their relative to be admitted, it is generally agreed to be best practice for this role to be performed by ASWs. Legal duties and powers to act under the MHA 1983 have to be weighed carefully against rights of individuals under The Human Rights Act 1998. A new Mental Health bill is currently being formulated and amongst the changes and proposals is for the role currently filled solely by ASWs to be extended to include other 'suitably qualified' mental health professionals. If implemented this would allow community mental health nurses, psychologists and community occupational therapists as well as social workers to apply for the admission of a patient under the Act.

Currently ASWs are responsible for co-ordinating assessments conducted under the MHA. They must respond to requests from a patient's nearest relative to assess people under the act. Having interviewed the patient in a 'suitable manner', preferably with two doctors, and having satisfied themselves that 'in all the circumstances of the case' (MHA section 13) the patient should be admitted to hospital, the ASW needs to oversee the necessary arrangements to ensure that this is done. The ASW is obliged to ensure that the patient is treated in the 'least restrictive' manner possible (Jones, 2002). This means that they should be allowed to be admitted to hospital as a voluntary/informal patient if they have the necessary capacity to understand and give fully informed consent. If they need to be admitted compulsorily against their expressed wishes (sectioned) then the section of the act used (usually section 2, primarily for assessment and detention for up to 28 days, or section 3, primarily for treatment and detention for up to six months) should be the least restrictive possible in the circumstances. In extreme and urgent cases if it proves impossible to find two suitably qualified doctors to attend for an assessment an ASW may apply with only one medical recommendation. The patient can then be detained for up to 72 hours whilst the second medical recommendation required under section 2 is provided. The role of the ASW is complex and calls for a sensitive and sophisticated balancing of needs, rights, responsibilities, risks and predicted dangers (Sheppard, 1990; The Social Services Inspectorate, 2001; Smith, 2001a).

A common requirement of EDT work is to respond to requests for assessment under the MHA following the detention by police of people under section 136 of the Act. This section empowers a police constable to remove to a place of safety (usually a police station or a hospital), any person found in a place to which the public have access, 'who appears to him to be suffering from mental disorder and to be in immediate need of care or control'. Whereas section 135 of the Act concerns powers of entry into private dwellings, authorised by a magistrate's warrant, section 136 has relevance to 'public places' and does not require a warrant for arrest. Examples of people taken to a place of safety under this section include those found apparently contemplating suicide on railway bridges and at the top of high car parks, those found wandering without any apparent recollection of who they are or where they come from and those acting in socially unacceptable ways in public places when mental disorder is thought to be the cause of this behaviour.

The choice of a suitable place of safety is likely to be determined by the nature and manifestations of the disorder – those believed to be a danger to themselves are more likely to be taken to a hospital, while those believed to be a potential danger to others are more likely to be taken to a police station. Jointly agreed local policies and protocols should determine the handling of individual cases although there may still be disputes about where is the most appropriate place, particularly if the person concerned has been drinking alcohol or is under the influence of mind-altering substances. Section 1 of the MHA states that people should not be detained under it, 'by reason only of . . . dependence on alcohol or drugs'. It is therefore important that people are sober and sufficiently clear of mind-altering substances when being assessed so that their 'true' underlying mental state is apparent, independent of the influences of such substances.

Responding to requests to assess people under section 136 of the MHA out of hours can account for over 50 per cent of MHA assessments carried out by EDTs. Other assessments conducted on hospital in-patients include those of 'conversions' from section 2 to 3, and of section 5(2) when a doctor has put a temporary (maximum 72 hours) holding order on a previously informal patient who has attempted to leave the ward and who is thought still to be at too great a risk to do so. Other assessments may be conducted in hospital accident and emergency departments. All other assessments concern people in the community. These can present organisational difficulties, particularly if a police presence is thought to be necessary before someone can be assessed safely, or if suitable doctors are not available, or if there are long delays in waiting for an ambulance once an assessment has been completed and an application made (Smith, 2001a). Because the MHA does not have a lower age limit it is possible that assessments may be requested on anyone of any age, including children and young people.

Mental Health Act Assessments: children

The Children Act 1989 defines anyone aged under 18 as a child. While children as young as four are thought to be capable of having psychotic states (Rustin et al., 1997) occurrences of these are comparatively rare. Recently, however, some commentators have observed an increasing tendency towards, 'the psychiatrization of everything' whereby, 'more people seem to be diagnosed as suffering from more psychiatric disorders than ever'. (Porter, 2002: 214). In the case of children this is apparent in the increasingly common diagnosis attention-deficit-hyperactivity-disorder and prescribed medication (Ritalin) for this. Families and others may welcome the relief that comes from having a specific diagnosis and the hope afforded by effective treatment. Others, however, are often sceptical, claiming that this 'recently-discovered' condition merely dresses naughty and boisterous children in a different set of the emperor's new clothes. However, some parents and carers do contact EDTs apparently at the mercy of their infants. One mother called, sounding panic stricken, asking for advice because her two year-old was 'walking around, threatening me with a knife'. Sometimes EDT workers are told that a difficult child 'must be mad' and so needs to be treated by way of psychiatric rather than general children's services. While it may be easier to encourage parents and carers of younger children to seek help through appropriate daytime preventative services such as Child Mental Health teams there can be pressure to consider assessments under the MHA and 'sectioning' for adolescents.

Chapter 2 considers issues relevant to working with adolescence as a stage of life and the recent concerns about high rates of self-harming and suicidal behaviours during this vulnerable period. EDTs which cover areas having specialist adolescent mental health facilities will be likely to be particularly busy with doing assessments relating to this service user group, since conversions from one section to another are often requested. The police may have attended a domestic dispute which has involved a breach of the peace or criminal damage and then contact EDT to ask that an adolescent involved be assessed under mental health, rather than child care legislation. Children's homes or foster carers can request assessments under the MHA if they believe that behaviours might be caused primarily by mental disorder rather than anger, delinquency, deviancy or substance abuse.

When assessing young people it is often difficult to distinguish between mental illness, learning disability, substance abuse and criminality. At 10.00 p.m. one night EDT was called to attend a situation involving a 16-year-old adolescent, known to have a mild learning disability, who had smashed up his bedroom and all his possessions. His mother said he had experienced and shown his frustration on several previous occasions but that on this particular night he had behaved in an unusually extreme and disturbed manner. She thought that he may have been under the influence of drugs but was not sure of details and had no evidence to confirm this view. She wondered whether he might be mentally ill. He had completely destroyed his favourite games and electrical equipment including expensive gifts from his parents and things he had himself saved up to buy. There had been a row and he had fought with his father. His mother felt that her loyalties were divided between her son and her husband but said that, on balance, her priorities were with her husband and so would not allow her son to remain living at home.

The young man was being held at the police station because of the criminal damage and his father was at the same station for having assaulted his son. This situation demonstrates the extreme difficulties faced by an EDT when there are no suitable resources available for young people of this age, particularly if they have an associated mental health problem or learning disability. It also highlights the shortfalls in the minimal staffing levels that EDTs frequently work with since only one EDT worker was on duty when this referral was received. There was a potential need for an appropriate adult to attend an interview with the young man under The Police and Criminal Evidence Act 1984 if he was to be interviewed about the criminal damage (his parents could not attend being the 'aggrieved' party since the damage had been done to their house). There was also the possibility that the police doctor would see him and subsequently request assessment under the MHA. If the mother remained adamant that she would not allow him back home and he was thought not to be mentally ill there would then be the need to explore placement possibilities, even though it was highly unlikely that there would be any suitable ones immediately available. If a placement were to be found, documentation would need to be completed and transport (with suitable escort) arranged. The first course of action was to discuss the situation in more detail with the mother to see if she could be persuaded to change her mind and have her son back home, at least until the next working day. It would be desirable to visit and discuss this with her face-to-face. If this were to be done there were extra risk assessment considerations. She might be very angry, whilst her husband could return home from the police station feeling angry and frustrated and might direct these feelings at social workers found in his house.

No potential placements were found to be available anywhere but this situation was eventually resolved when an EDT sessional worker agreed to work additional hours and to accompany the EDT worker on a visit to the young man's mother. Several hours had elapsed since the original referral and by then everyone had been able to reflect upon the course of events and how they felt about them. The mother showed the two workers the damage which her son had caused to the house and talked of her sadness and anger at his having destroyed the presents she had worked hard to buy for him. Sometimes this 'bearing witness' aspect of the EDT role can help to achieve movement in previously 'stuck' situations. When EDT workers do not leave the office to visit situations, service users can feel angry that their difficulties are being dealt with only by 'remote control' over the telephone. They believe that if only workers would come and see for themselves they would not and could not maintain such a dispassionate detachment when confronted with the evidence. Service users will therefore often attempt to insist, cajole or implore EDT workers to come and 'see' the difficulties for themselves. While, as on this occasion, this may sometimes be a useful strategy, making a visit might otherwise be construed as offering people false hope that EDT will be able to 'do' more about a problem than they really can.

The workers attempted to acknowledge the mother's distress about what had happened and, at the same time, to appeal to those parts of her that clearly still loved and cared about her son. They told her of the people they had spoken with, the options they had explored, and explained why (now at just past midnight) it was not possible to try anywhere else before the next working day. Having ascertained that all parties concerned had calmed down sufficiently and agreed to live together peacefully until the next working day it was eventually agreed that father and son would both return home from the police station and that the situation would be followed up by the daytime team the next working day. This case illustrates the value for EDTs to be able to call in additional help at times of peak demand and particular need. Because the timing of these needs is unknown the flexibility of having additional staff available when required is essential for delivering an effective and appropriate response.

As for adult assessments, concerns for the mental health of children and young people are not so much that they have been an actual or potential danger to others, but that they are thought to be a danger to themselves. Rates of self-harm and suicide in adolescence are rising (Smith, 2002) and there are particular concerns for young people who live in institutional settings since self-harming behaviours often have an infectious or contagious quality. This means that if one person in a unit starts to harm themselves, others may quickly imitate. On one occasion an EDT worker was called to assess three young people all taken together to a police station as a place of safety. One, with a history of self-harming attempts, had expressed to fellow residents her intention of throwing herself from a high bridge. Two other young residents who were also feeling depressed said they would join her. The three of them had made a pact to jump together but had been intercepted by the police. Such assessments prove difficult for EDT workers who have limited, if any, access to the histories and complex multi-faceted factors contributing to the current situation. EDT workers need to find out from appropriate others as much information as they can during the limited time available. Whatever they discover, however, they know that they are seeing only the tip of an iceberg.

While 'sectioning' people of any age is a serious matter, never to be undertaken lightly, children and young people, by definition, will usually have to live for even longer with the stigma and disadvantages of being sectioned than their older counterparts will. Therefore, while recognising that on occasions this course of action will still sometimes be necessary, EDT workers should make all reasonable attempts to uncover relevant information so that least restrictive alternatives can be employed whenever possible. Balancing the desire to acknowledge and respect people's rights to autonomy and self-determination while simultaneously keeping them safe from their capacity for self-destruction entails walking a thin line. This holds true for adults as well as for children as illustrated by the following case example.

Mental Health Act Assessments: adults

An Asian man aged 34 was experiencing difficulties in his marriage and began an affair. He became distressed about his life in general and rented a hotel room for a few nights in order to clear some time and space in which to think. He felt guilty about leaving his wife and young children for a new partner but was unhappy and felt unfulfilled within his marriage. While staying at the hotel he decided that he wanted to die and drank some anti-freeze. After having done so he became concerned about the possible consequences of this, and called one of his brothers who took him directly to the local accident and emergency department. He was assessed there by the EDT duty ASW and two doctors. Five family members were already present with him, and more continued to arrive as the assessment progressed. Each wanted the stigma of being sectioned to be avoided and were concerned how a diagnosis of mental illness might affect his hitherto successful career as a solicitor. They attempted to persuade him to agree to voluntary admission and appropriate treatment but he would do neither and maintained a consistent and determined resistance despite their pleading. Each time a new family member arrived they would provide more information and thus augment the details relating to the background and context of the man's life.

The man steadfastly refused to change his mind and his family were surprised at the strength of his resistance. They seemed embarrassed that the details of his affair and suicide attempt had become known in the way that they had done. The EDT worker and doctors thought that they had no option other than to section this man since he was clearly still a danger to himself and was unwilling to accept help on a voluntary basis. This case illustrates how it might not be considered safe to pursue a less restrictive alternative even when plentiful background information is available and there is considerable willingness to provide support within an extended family network.

Sometimes people are more of a risk to others than they are to themselves. The wife of a young man with a well-documented mental health history, and who had served a custodial sentence following a frenzied attack on a young woman, reported concerns about him. He had stopped taking his anti-psychotic medication and had become increasingly preoccupied with trying to find parallels between his own life and the lives of famous religious teachers. She feared that he was becoming increasingly unwell and reported that he had thrown her against the kitchen wall and threatened her with violence. She said she feared for her own safety and for that of their young child. She had left him and gone to a woman's refuge for a short time but had later returned to him. She requested an urgent assessment.

The EDT worker consulted the duty psychiatrist and both agreed that this was a high-risk situation that should be visited only with an appropriate police attendance. The EDT worker contacted the wife again and discussed more details with her. She said that her husband was not particularly disturbed or thought to be potentially violent that night. It therefore seemed that this situation could be allowed to wait until the next working day when the man could be referred for assessment to his own general practitioner and to a psychiatrist who knew them. It is good practice whenever possible for people to be assessed under the MHA by professionals who actually know them because they are able to evaluate the thoughts and behaviours which they are observing and assessing within the context of their previous knowledge of that person. The wife said that if necessary she and her child could stay overnight with friends or family, away from her husband. She was advised to call the police if she was in need of immediate assistance at any time throughout the night and was told that the referral would be passed on to the daytime ASW. The EDT worker notified the police of his discussions with the wife so that they would know of the situation and be able to respond appropriately should they be called. This was a case where EDTs response was to assess the risks within the situation, 'hold' it through the night having built in essential safety measures, and not intervene hoping that the husband would receive a more appropriate assessment from those who knew him the following day.

General practitioners and psychiatrists may not always be available in daytime hours so assessments, are sometimes left until the end of the day. Doctors may prefer to do them in the early evening after they have finished surgeries and daytime rota commitments. This is an inconvenient time for EDTs however because they are just beginning duty then and are likely to have calls, faxes and e-mails to respond to and prioritise. This situation could be improved if Community Mental Health teams were able to extend their hours of work to include early evenings.

Over recent years most general practitioners have provided their out of hours cover by joining together in cooperatives whereby they cover for one another's surgeries. This means that individual doctors are on duty less frequently but serve a larger area. It also means that covering doctors are unlikely to know people referred for assessment under the MHA and this is not in the patient's best interests. Because covering doctors can know only what they are told and do not have comprehensive access to a patient's full medical history, they often have to act on the basis of incomplete knowledge. Their options are limited; they can listen, advise, prescribe medication, visit, and/or request a MHA assessment if they believe one to be indicated. Few general practitioners are especially approved to assess patients under section 12 of the MHA and most prefer to pass this responsibility on to others who have been trained for this role. General practitioners may therefore contact EDT ASWs and ask them to assess situations which they have encountered to determine whether, or not, a MHA assessment is necessary.

Sometimes, relatively innocuous situations may escalate and appear to be worse than they are. On one occasion, a covering general practitioner contacted EDT and requested a MHA for a young woman whom he described as experiencing religious mania. He said she had locked her husband out of their house and was acting oddly with their three children, repeatedly talking about God and Satan and waking them up at 3.00 a.m. to read them stories from the Bible. The doctor explained that his own knowledge of the situation was indirect and partial but that his colleague had visited the woman earlier in the day and prescribed some anti-psychotic medication which she had refused to take. He saw no alternative but to request a MHA assessment. The EDT duty ASW telephoned the woman's husband as the nearest relative to discuss the situation with him. It was apparent from what the husband said that his wife was also in the same room with him so after a while the EDT worker was able to speak to the woman herself. After talking for about half an hour it was apparent to the EDT worker that whatever was wrong with that young woman there was also much about her that was cognitively intact and mentally appropriate. He wondered whether her reported illness had become exaggerated since it had been passed between a succession of people, none of whom knew her well. Having completed a risk assessment and discussed the matter with a colleague, the worker decided to visit to talk with the couple face-to-face.

During his visit he learnt that both had experienced a number of stressful life events recently. The husband had been made redundant, the wife feared cancer, neither had been sleeping well, their three young children had been demanding and one had been seriously ill. The timing of all of this had coincided with the anniversary of a painful bereavement. The more the EDT worker listened to them the more reasonable and appropriate to their circumstances the responses seemed. The couple had a strong religious faith but did not talk of this in a delusional or inappropriate way. The wife had not actually shut the husband out of their house but there had been a misunderstanding about keys, which had become reported as her locking him out and her and the children in. They had been up at unsociable hours because illness had disrupted their sleep patterns and the mother had been reading to the children to calm and comfort them.

The social worker's assessment was that this was not a mental health crisis at all but an understandable and rational reaction to a succession of distressing life events which were affecting all family members. Having recommended various daytime provisions which might be usefully explored later, the social worker left and informed the covering doctor's service of the outcome of his visit. Giving the couple concerned time to explore, talk through and come to understand something of how their recent difficulties had provided a containment of the complex situation which could otherwise have escalated into a crisis. Had the woman been sectioned unnecessarily, the subsequent negative repercussions for herself and her family could have been considerable. The couple were not aware of the course of events they had set in motion by their style of communicating their distress. Part of the social worker's purpose in visiting was to explain to them how the system worked and to warn of the likely consequences of their behaviours if they continued to express themselves in their previous manner. The need to differentiate between the 'real' crises when severe mental illness poses a genuine threat to life and livelihood and the pseudo crises which appear falsely to require medical intervention is a permanent dilemma for those doing mental health work. This difficulty applies to both younger and older people alike.

Mental Health Act Assessments: older people

In the previous examples further information about service users was obtained by speaking directly with them or with people who knew them, and also by consulting available records. In some instances, however, this is not possible. The police may find an older person walking down a road in the early hours of the morning having no apparent recollection of who they are or where they come from. Repeated questioning may not provide any relevant information and arrangements will need to be made to find suitable overnight accommodation so that more detailed enquiries can be made the following day.

Older people living alone and suffering from dementia may leave their accommodation in the night and go out walking, often without suitable clothes or any personal identification. If found and asked where they were intending to go they may have forgotten or may provide an address from a childhood memory which no longer exists as they remember it. Those being looked after by informal carers or by professional support services may develop paranoid beliefs that the people trying to look after them are actually there to harm them, perhaps poison them, steal from them or to lie to them. They may therefore become suspicious and aggressive, perhaps not recognising even partners they have lived with for decades. Such behaviours are painfully distressing for people who have devoted themselves to caring for their loved ones and those carers may contact EDT for support and advice. Despite recent developments in community based services it is often not possible to increase the level of service provided out of hours and at short notice so it may sometimes be necessary to consider a MHA assessment.

Responding to callers who have developed delusional ideas or who have little short-term memory can pose difficulties for EDT workers. Sometimes it may be impossible, to ascertain over the telephone where the truth lies in a service user's insistence that there are problems, for example, with the plumbing. There might be actual problems with the plumbing whereas sometimes their perception serves as the external focus for a confused and delusional belief system. The patience of EDT workers was tested repeatedly over several weekends when one caller who had virtually no short-term memory kept telephoning to insist that her meals on wheels had not arrived. Having called EDT she forgot that she had done so and called again, only a few minutes later. Even after her meal had arrived and been eaten she forgot this too and called EDT again to report that it still had not been delivered. While this behaviour, in itself, does not merit a MHA assessment the potential dangers of the underlying forgetfulness and lack of short-term memory (such as leaving the gas on or the front door open) need to be addressed and a MHA assessment might be considered to be necessary.

A delusional belief system that has been developing and operating for some time may suddenly cause problems at night or over a weekend and then require an immediate response. An example of this concerns an older person who lived alone and who developed increasingly paranoid ideas about her neighbour. She had become convinced that if she were to turn on any electrical switch in her own house then her neighbour would transmit magical dust between their houses and that this dust would come down through the light fittings and blind her. Because of this belief she would not turn on any switches for light or heating throughout the winter months. She lived in fear with her dogs, enduring the cold and darkness because she did not feel sufficiently safe to heat any food or water. She drew attention to her delusional perceptions when she attacked her neighbour in the belief that her mail was being intercepted and tampered with. On discovering her circumstances the duty ASW arranged a MHA assessment, following which she was sectioned and the dogs were kennelled.

Darkness and night frequently provide a context which enhances the power of older people's delusions. One older man was convinced that aliens had landed in his back yard and were transporting unsuspecting people away to other planets and galaxies. His beliefs seemed to be totally unfounded until a community worker pointed out that he lived near to a depot which dispatched washing machines. From his bedroom window the man could look out on a courtyard in which washing machines were loaded into lorries at night. The people loading the gleaming white washing machines into containers, illuminated by stark bright yellow lights in the car park, appeared to be part of an alien operation to someone who saw things that way.

Having considered how EDTs may respond to the various mental health problems experienced by people of different ages this chapter now concludes with some recommendations for good practice for mental health work out of hours.

Recommendations for good practice in mental health work

- Callers who essentially want to talk and be listened to and who do not constitute a mental health emergency should be directed to different appropriate resources.
- EDTs are not the best service to make check calls to vulnerable service users who are thought to need such calls, and this should be recognised by daytime workers.
- Crisis intervention and home treatment teams should be available when required to support and complement the services available from EDTs.
- The influence of mind-altering substances needs to be allowed for, and the effects of these substances should not be mistaken for mental illness.
- EDT workers need to avoid the opposite dangers of under and over-reaction. The trivial will not meet with an over-reaction while the apparently trivial but actually serious should be recognised as such.
- Agreed, tried and tested protocols and procedures with partner agencies should be in place. In particular these are important for section 136 of the MHA.
- Risk assessments should be carefully thought through, discussed and recorded.

- Least restrictive alternatives should be promoted whenever possible, but accurate recognition is essential in instances when compulsion may be needed.
- An appropriate balance is to be struck between allowing people's rights to autonomy and the protection of individuals from themselves and from others.
- Situations should be held and contained when possible and untimely and inappropriate interventions should be resisted.
- Firm and decisive action must be forthcoming when this is warranted.
- Appropriate and full information should be made available to EDTs from daytime teams including comprehensive risk assessments when available.

CHAPTER 4

Vulnerable adults

This chapter begins with an outline of the role of the appropriate adult working with vulnerable adults under the Police and Criminal Evidence Act (PACE) 1984. The limitations and powers of this role are discussed. The importance of partnership working is highlighted in cases where there is a need to return vulnerable adults to their home area, which may be hundreds of miles away, when no one agency is clearly responsible to perform this task. The needs of vulnerable adults living in community settings and their carers are then considered. The difficulties of dealing with repeat callers who forget they have called and of assessing the likely level of risk posed by confused people are then debated. The need for effective partnership with the police is highlighted throughout. Consideration is given to the needs of those requiring money or emergency housing out of normal office hours and also to those of victims of domestic violence. Finally, the chapter ends with some recommendations for good practice.

Attending PACE interviews with vulnerable adults

The codes of practice for the Police and Criminal Evidence Act (PACE) 1984 (Part C, annex E.1) state, 'If an officer has any suspicion or is told in good faith that a person of any age, whether or not in custody, may be suffering from mental disorder or be mentally handicapped, or cannot understand the significance of questions put to him or his replies, then he shall be treated as a mentally disordered or mentally handicapped person'. A person whom the police want to interview and who fits these criteria needs to be accompanied by an 'appropriate adult'. Such an adult is defined as being a relative or guardian or 'someone who has experience of dealing with mentally disordered or mentally handicapped persons but is not a police officer or employed by the police'. When such persons are not available the role may be fulfilled by any responsible adult aged 18 or over who is not a police officer or employed by the police. EDT workers might therefore be asked to act in the role of appropriate adult for potentially vulnerable adults since they have experience of dealing with mentally disordered or mentally handicapped persons and are not employed by the police.

The appropriate adult '. . . is not expected to act simply as an observer . . . the purposes of his presence are, first to advise the person being questioned and to observe whether or not the interview is being conducted properly and fairly, and secondly, to facilitate communication with the person being interviewed' (Codes of practice: C 11.16). The role of the appropriate adult therefore differs from that of the approved social worker (discussed in Chapter 3) who is called to assess people under The Mental Health Act 1983. The appropriate adult's role is with those who are suspected of having committed a criminal offence and is essentially that of a caring parent – to check that detainees are not hungry or thirsty and feel sufficiently physically and mentally well to do justice to themselves in an interview. A detainee's capacity for being interviewed is determined before an official interview starts, and should be continually reviewed throughout the process. Having initially satisfied himself that a detainee is able to understand what is being asked, an appropriate adult may revise this view as the interview progresses and request that it be terminated at any time if he deems this to be necessary.

The appropriate adult should not advise detainees on legal matters because this is the province of the solicitor who should also be present at interview or have been contacted by telephone. It is also inadvisable for the appropriate adult to hear the detainee's account of the alleged offence prior to interview as they may be obliged to pass on certain information which solicitors might choose to keep confidential within the context of their professional role. By not only observing the interview but also helping to facilitate communication and satisfying themselves that interviews are conducted properly and fairly, appropriate adults provide both protection for detainees being interviewed and endorsement of the officers doing the interviewing. (For a fuller discussion of the appropriate adult role see Littlechild, 1996.)

Knowing whether or not someone should be interviewed under mental health or criminal legislation can be a fine matter of judgement and situations may change. Someone might first be interviewed about an alleged offence in the presence of an appropriate adult but later it becomes apparent that they are less mentally well than was first thought so that they may then be considered to be in need of assessment under the Mental Health Act 1983. Conversely, someone may be assessed initially under the Mental Health Act and, if not detained under this legislation, be considered fit for interview about an alleged criminal offence. Police doctors will often be requested to determine which route the assessment/interview should take. While it is the case that mentally ill people should not be expected to have the same accountability for criminal acts as people who are not mentally ill, it is also the case that people who are not mentally ill should not employ mental illness as a defence against criminal accusations.

In the case of people with learning disabilities EDT workers may be asked to attend interviews as appropriate adults for a wide range of reasons. At one extreme there are the comparatively trivial crimes such as repeated minor thefts of sweets from a supermarket. At the other extreme are occasions when a person is suspected of murder. The different ways in which people can be affected by being in a police custody area need to be recognised. A person with a learning disability may begin their time in custody with an air of brash bravado, attempting humour, and generally creating an impression that they are unconcerned and unaffected by their surroundings. As time goes on, however, and the inevitable paperwork and various delays contribute to hours passing, their demeanour may change and they become noticeably more distressed the longer they are there. Custody areas, by definition, need to be secure, and so they can be uncomfortable environments for those prone to claustrophobia or who worry about being locked up in confined spaces. Noisy, drunk or violent people may be brought in who cause detainees further worry. A possible danger here is that people may 'confess to anything' simply because they think this will help them to get away from the custody area as quickly as possible and the appropriate adult needs to aware of this.

If a detainee suspected of murder is first questioned on a Friday night or at the beginning of a bank holiday weekend the process might go on for several days and could involve a number of different EDT workers acting as appropriate adults for the same detainee. A suspect may become tearful in response to a repeated line of questioning and it can be hard to know whether this is because of an un-confessed guilt or because of a fear that, although innocent, they might be found to be guilty. It is difficult to know what constitutes a 'proper and fair' interview in these circumstances. Police officers may interpret tears as a sign that they are getting somewhere important whereas appropriate adults and solicitors might interpret those same tears as being the result of oppressive questioning. In an ideal world police officers, appropriate adults and solicitors will work in partnership to discuss, from their different perspectives and in the context of the requirements of PACE, what they see to be in the best interests of the detainee. In practice sides can sometimes be taken and polarised thinking of 'us and them' mentalities may develop.

When EDT workers have completed their attendance at an interview in their role as appropriate adult the issue of how someone is going to get home might arise. If a person lives fairly near to the police station, has money, and public transport is running there is no problem. If they live miles away in another area and do not have money sufficient to return home the matter will need discussion. This issue applies similarly to other vulnerable adults who come to the attention of EDT and the police out of hours.

Returning vulnerable adults home

Whereas social workers used to routinely transport service users as part of their work with them, following a number of serious mishaps and increasingly restrictive health and safety legislation (see Chapter 6) they are now less likely to do so. Policies in many areas will stipulate that if workers do transport service users they need to have appropriate insurance cover and that they should do so only if accompanied by an escort. As well as helping to ensure the physical safety of drivers, an escort can act as a witness in cases where an allegation may be made. Some vulnerable adults have made allegations of abuse against others and workers need to recognise that they themselves might be vulnerable to such allegations. They therefore need to ensure that protective measures are in place. The police may or may not be prepared to return home someone who has been interviewed depending on the circumstances of the case and how busy they are with other work. Someone else therefore, might need to take responsibility. Because people have been deemed sufficiently vulnerable to require an appropriate adult in the first place their possible need for assistance in getting home should be recognised when this is necessary. EDT workers can sometimes assist with this by accompanying people to public transport and paying their fare or providing a travel warrant once there. Problems arise if there is no suitable public transport running at the time when it is needed such as over a bank holiday weekend or late at night. These difficulties can only be resolved by detailed and time-consuming negotiations with the various parties involved as shown below.

A young woman with a mild learning disability left the area she lived in 'voluntarily' to be with a man who was a schedule one sex offender. She travelled 600 miles with him after which he simply left her alone to fend for herself one Sunday. The police picked her up at 10.00 a.m. and began discussing the question of her return with the covering EDT worker. Contact was made with her family who were willing to do all they could to assist her return but they were not able to find anyone who could come and collect her. The police, understandably, wanted her out of the police station as quickly as possible but there was nowhere obvious for her to go and wait while her return home was discussed and organised. Most residential units run on minimal staffing levels at weekends and, because of the current emphasis on risk assessment (see Chapter 6), are extremely reluctant to take responsibility for someone they know very little about. In any event, few units are likely to have a vacancy.

The young woman's family were also concerned about her ability to travel anywhere alone, without an escort. They said that her disability was such that she gave the impression of being more capable than she actually was and that she would be extremely worried travelling on her own since she had never done so previously. This presented considerable difficulties for the local EDT workers involved, as there was no one employed with a responsibility, let alone availability, to accompany her 600 miles home in an escorting role! According to the EDT covering her home area she was not known to her local social services. In theory, therefore, no one was responsible for returning her home, yet she could not arrange this for herself. The service user waited at the police station while airports, coach, rail and taxi services were contacted and nothing seemed possible. Several airlines wanted proof of identity before they would accept a booking and this could not be provided.

The situation was eventually resolved by a residential unit eventually agreeing to take her for the night at 10 p.m. and an airline agreeing to accept a booking for her without proof of identity. The following morning a taxi was arranged to take her to the airport and the local police force escorted her from the taxi and on to the plane where she was looked after by cabin staff. Her family met her on arrival.

This one case had required hours of work by the police, EDT and the residential staff who fortunately had both a spare bed for the night and the willingness to take in a complete stranger. It shows that someone, or some service, needed to be responsible for the young woman but not who or how, or from what budget. The case is a good example of the partnership approach (see

Chapter 8) and resourcefulness needed out of hours when, despite the various components of supportive networks, there is no precedent, no clearly defined accountability and no obvious way forward.

On other occasions EDT may be contacted by service users, known to have a learning disability, from an accident and emergency department of a hospital saying that they need to get home, that there is no available public transport, or that they have no money to do so. Procedures agreed with daytime workers are helpful in such instances as these cases raise the question of assessing the extent of someone's disability or vulnerability. If they are thought to be sufficiently vulnerable and genuinely in need, a taxi may be authorised; if they are not there may be nothing that can be done to help. To be too helpful in such instances can sometimes set an unhelpful precedent in the mind of the service user and, unintentionally, encourage them to think that this assistance can be provided for them on a regular basis.

Other problems faced by EDTs when working with vulnerable adults are not so much about returning people home but responding to their needs while at their home.

Needs of vulnerable adults living in community settings

EDTs tend to work with physically disabled adults relatively little. Very disabled adults are more likely to receive care from health service professionals, such as occupational therapists and district nurses, who provide and monitor the functioning of necessary equipment aids and appliances. Occasionally though, an EDT might be called about the malfunctioning of an important piece of equipment and need to decide with the caller about how to contact the relevant people who can help with its repair. EDTs are more likely to routinely deal with people with a learning disability.

The nature of some people's learning disability can be such that precise order, routine and familiarity are of the greatest importance to them. Therefore, if someone they live with uses the washing machine when it was not 'their turn' or rearranges the furniture in a way or at a time that the caller finds unacceptable, this is perceived by them as being a 'genuine emergency'. For a busy EDT worker, who may also be dealing with requests for mental health act assessments or child protection referrals, the washing machine rota may not appear to be a problem of the same order. It is important, however, that these referrals are taken seriously and that the distress of the situation to the caller is recognised. If they are not, that distress might escalate so that a more serious crisis is provoked with undesirable repercussions, both for them, and the people they live with.

Sometimes people with a learning disability demonstrate very regressed behaviour and will demand and cry for their familiar community worker as a young child cries for its mother. Again, it is helpful for EDT workers to know from daytime workers what helps to calm these callers down in these circumstances. If callers feel that their distress has been recognised and 'heard' they are often able to calm down and regain their composure and equilibrium. Sometimes, their needs are more practical, for example for a plumber or electrician, and EDTs are helped by being provided with a list of approved contractors who can be contacted in these instances.

Sometimes normally mentally well adults can be made vulnerable by adverse circumstances. One Sunday evening a man called EDT to report that he had returned home from some time away to find that his house, along with several others in his street, had been struck by lightning and ravaged by fire. He said he had found the EDT telephone number in the directory and needed help with the emergency he now faced. He talked in a fast and muddled way, at times he was almost incoherent. He said that the front of his house had been virtually destroyed and there were piles of rubble, damaged objects and exposed wires everywhere. He was reluctant to leave his property for fear of theft and said he had contacted both the police and his insurance company but neither had been of any help to him. He said his house had been cordoned off with tape and that having managed to get to sleep the previous night he had awoken to find people walking around his property and shining torches at him through the darkness. He later discovered these people to be the police. The word picture he painted sounded bizarre and surreal. The EDT worker taking the call could not decide if she was listening to a hoax, the result of an alcohol or drug induced state, the manifestations of a mental illness or breakdown, or a fundamentally accurate description of a real though unusual and particularly stressful state of affairs.

The difficulty in making sense of and dealing with the call was compounded by the man's repeated question, 'And where is the brigadier? Where is the brigadier now that I need him here?' This question made no sense to the EDT worker whilst taking the call and the man was unable to or unwilling to explain what he meant by it. He was clearly in considerable distress, however, and the worker encouraged him to talk further about his circumstances and difficulties. As he talked further the man became calmer, more rational and more appropriately thoughtful.

The EDT worker offered to contact the man's insurance company for him to ask what could be done. Although the man said he had already contacted the insurance company himself the worker reasoned that this was all she could *do* for him. Even if nothing was achieved by doing so and even if nothing new was discovered as a result, at least the man would know that the worker had 'heard' what he had said and tried to help him. This, in itself, might make a difference. The EDT worker contacted the insurance company who advised that the man should secure his property the best he could and stay in a local hotel at their expense while the situation could be investigated. On calling the man back the EDT worker found him calmer still. He had thought things through and decided that he would go and stay in a hotel, or maybe with a friend, until he could sort things out. When saying goodbye he sounded far more realistic, composed and ordered than he had done at the beginning of the call.

Sometime after dealing with this call the EDT worker involved was discussing it with a colleague who suggested that in referring to the brigadier the man may have been recalling a recently-shown television documentary on seal culling. The EDT worker responding to the man had not seen this documentary but apparently a number of seals were being culled in a situation of great distress, disorder and confusion. Into this setting had stepped a brigadier who appeared to know precisely what needed to be done and how to do it. He took charge of the situation where-after order and efficient organisation took the place of the previous chaos. The brigadier's extreme composure and 'taking charge' in disorder and confusion had, apparently, made a powerful impression on many viewers of the programme. It may have been that in his distress, loss and incomprehension the man calling EDT had retained the image of the brigadier as personifying the ultimate calm management in the face of chaos but could not articulate this at the time. He may have been asking, both himself and the EDT worker, where was the (equivalent) brigadier for him, in his circumstances, when he needed him, but had been able to formulate this question only in a dream-like rather than reality-based manner. If this is what had been influencing him it serves as a reminder for EDT workers to not be dismissive of communications which may not make sense at the time. At times of crisis and trauma emotional 'reality' is likely to become split off from cognitive, external reality. Meanings may become apparent later and only after reflection, discussion and hindsight.

Sometimes the EDT's role with vulnerable adults also entails working closely with those who care for such adults in a personal or professional capacity.

Working with vulnerable adults and their carers

Many vulnerable adults of various ages can live in community settings only because of considerable support packages comprising different health and social care professionals performing complementary roles, together with the good will and dedication of other family members, known as 'informal carers'. The demands made on informal carers can vary considerably ranging from those made by relatively younger people with manic depression or schizophrenia to those made by older people with dementia. For some carers the demands are such that they feel they are living a '36-hour day' (Mace et al., 1985). Informal carers might be motivated by a combination of love and duty but may also find their task daunting in the extreme when, despite their best efforts, the cared for person engages in reckless spending sprees, becomes sexually promiscuous or aggressive, or does not even recognise the carer with whom they have lived for many years.

Informal carers might be supported by carers and support groups which meet on a planned basis and by a network of friends established through these groups but there is little provision available for them out of hours at short notice. Although EDT workers can talk through the immediate difficulties encountered and instigate assessments for possible admission into such resources as are available they can often do little more than this. Carers may believe that there is more support available out of hours than there actually is and EDT representatives can talk helpfully to carers and support groups to inform them of their actual staffing levels, competing priorities and the reality of the limited support that exists. There are two particular advantages to doing this; carers are appraised of the reality of the limited provision that exists out of hours and, bearing this in mind, can inform EDT workers of how they can best be of help to them despite the constraints they work within.

Sometimes an older person will need admission into residential care or hospital because the carer who usually looks after them becomes ill or is admitted into hospital themselves. It is often only at such times that the extent and quality of care provided by informal carers becomes apparent. If older people need admission to a resource it is important that they are assessed as fully as possible and their needs discussed with covering general practitioners and other medical staff so that the right level of care can be provided for them. If people need nursing care they should not be admitted into residential facilities unable to provide this level of care. As with all aspects of service provision, budgets and daytime protocols and procedures will always need to be taken into account.

Carers of vulnerable adults may be faced with extremely difficult behaviours, feel the need for a break and yet be told that there is nowhere suitable available for respite care. This was the case for a mother of a 25-year-old young man who had a combined physical and learning disability along with a rare blood condition for which he was being treated with steroids. One of the side effects of the steroids was to make him very strong. The mother contacted EDT saying that her son had, 'blown his top' and was throwing furniture around. She had shut him in his bedroom and could hear him smashing up its contents. She had contacted her son's general practitioner who had visited and told her that there was no suitable available health provision that could help and that her son did not meet the criteria for assessment under the Mental Health Act.

After some thought the EDT worker taking the call decided to visit. He knew he had no resources to offer and that he was unable to *do* anything about the problem at all. However, he could actually meet the people concerned face-to-face, listen to and talk with them, attempt to calm things down and see, for himself, the damage that had been done. The mother described this as having been a helpful intervention when later interviewed as part of an EDT customer satisfaction survey (see Chapter 9):

He (the EDT worker) said that although it was beyond his power to do anything practical he would have liked to have done something. I found that very helpful and consoling at a time of crisis. He came in with a very non-judgemental attitude and had not bracketed (my son) in any category at all. In his summing up he said, 'Here is a very angry young man who is bored.' And my reaction was, 'Hallelujah! Here's someone who knows what he's talking about!' He came across as a very genuine person who would do a lot more if he could but who couldn't do these things because of the constraints he faced ... Although I can't remember him mentioning it at the time I had the impression that he had previous experience of working with disability because he was not condemning the disability and using that as a reason to section him or have him taken away by the police. He recognised the part played by the disability in making (my son) angry.

Once again, the value of *attention* from an EDT worker is apparent. By listening carefully and taking seriously what the mother said, doing the little he could by going to see the situation for himself, even in the knowledge that he had nothing to offer, the worker makes a difference. The mother refers to him as if he were a fair and impartial judge, 'In his summing up . . .' She respects his judgement, based on what he had seen, and finds this powerfully helpful, 'Hallelujah!' It is often a matter of fine judgement for EDT workers as to whether or not they visit service users as, sometimes, to do so when they have no resources to offer, might seem insensitive, even antagonistic, to those in need of respite. On this occasion, however, it seems that the worker read the situation well and was able to be, 'helpful and consoling at a time of crisis' by using himself as a resource and applying his skills in a respectful and appropriate manner.

Unfortunately the strain on some adults caring for others may be such that they abuse those in their care; physically, sexually, emotionally, financially or by neglect (Aguilera, 1998). EDTs therefore also need to know the details of adult abuse policies and be able to implement these. As with child protection (see Chapter 2) EDTs primary task is to work in partnership with the police to secure the immediate safety of people with whom they are involved whilst carefully recording any concerns requiring fuller investigation by daytime services at a later time.

Older people

The increasingly ageing population of the United Kingdom calls for enhanced understanding of the particular needs of this service user group (Biggs, 1993; Hughes, 1995; Jamieson et al., 1997). For many EDTs, work with older people accounts for some of their fastest growing referral rates in recent years. Use of increasingly sophisticated and capable community services comprising health and social care workers together with privately-run care agencies has been a feature of out of hours work in recent times. Even very frail older people can now receive effective support in their own homes. While these elaborate community support packages undoubtedly have advantages for those not wanting to relinquish the familiarity of their home for the perceived disadvantages of hospital or residential care they can sometimes be unreliable and prone to disruption. Carers' cars might not start in cold winter months. Hazardous road conditions can make driving unsafe. The unexpected illness of a carer due to start work early can cause considerable disruption in the lives of service users who are dependent on her coming in order to start their day. EDTs may receive calls from inconvenienced service users and be able to do nothing other than advise waiting until the problem can be resolved by the appropriate managers.

Older people suffering dementia pose particular difficulties (Kitwood, 1997) as the problems resulting from loss of short-term memory are profound and multi-faceted. An older person may call repeatedly (sometimes via the police or operator) having forgotten that they had called a few minutes previously and having no memory of a worker's response, however carefully worded! It can often be difficult for an EDT worker to assess whether a situation is of no real consequence or extremely serious. One older and disabled woman had a particularly fraught relationship with her only daughter and projected these difficulties onto EDT workers she spoke to. She would cry in plaintive tones down the telephone that her light had been left on by carers and needed turning off. Could EDT come around and do this for her? On other occasions she would claim to have dropped something and be unable to pick it up and be asking for assistance with this. It was extremely difficult to know when her needs were genuine and when not. She would also call her general practitioner, the police and fire service attempting to engage them with similar such requests and they would often contact EDT asking whether something could be done about her. Despite professionals meetings at which mutual difficulties were acknowledged and discussed there was nothing that could be done to stop the calls and each one called for a fresh evaluation of what an appropriate response should be. EDTs will often have several callers of this kind to deal with at various times. Although the individuals change (this older woman was eventually admitted into residential care) their place seems to be taken over by someone else. In this sense EDT workers feel that they are carrying a small caseload, despite their inconsistent shift patterns and crisis role, because of the frequency of calls from specific individuals who repeatedly make their needs well known.

Assessing possible risks that might be posed by and to older people with mental health problems can also be very difficult for EDT workers. One night the police visited an older woman having been asked to do so by a neighbour whom she had been troubling. They found very little food in her house and reported this, and their concern about her mental state, to an EDT worker and asked her to investigate. Checking computer records the worker found that this woman had expressed paranoid thoughts about her neighbours, saying that they wanted to kill her and that she may need to take defensive action against this threat by killing them first. A daytime worker had visited with the woman's general practitioner who had then made a referral to a psycho-geriatrician. The EDT worker called the woman who talked rationally and reasonably, explaining that she knew she had little food in the house but was going shopping tomorrow. She went on to say that she knew her neighbours were stealing her food and her money so she needed to be careful. She elaborated on this belief as the conversation progressed. Sensing the worker's questioning of her mental state she said, 'Oh, I'm of sound mind alright – it's just that people don't believe me'. She assured the worker that she was not going to act on her beliefs about her neighbours anymore that night and intended to go to bed. She agreed to further contact from the daytime worker the next day. The EDT worker decided it was sufficiently safe to take no further action that night and passed details on to the daytime worker for follow up. One of the difficulties of making such an assessment is that people in these circumstances are prone to forgetting what they have said previously or changing their mind very quickly. It was quite conceivable that a few minutes after putting the telephone down from talking to the EDT worker that the woman might leave her house in search of the neighbour she believed to be threatening her.

As mentioned previously, many older people have complex community support packages. Some supportive visits may be provided by private providers who have been commissioned to do so by care managers. If these providers are unable to gain entry to their clients and have concerns about their possible safety it raises the question of who should act and in what way. Usually the agency will have details of a client's next of kin and will inform them but if this is not available or there is no response they may be left feeling concerned and unsure of what to do. In such circumstances they might contact EDT as the representative of the employing agency. While EDT workers will be prepared to talk through the difficulties inherent in these kind of situations and try to help find a satisfactory way forward, they prefer that such agencies complete their own risk assessment and decide upon a course of action by themselves.

The choice to be made amounts to doing something further about the concern, such as making a follow up visit or telephone call, or trying again to contact the next of kin, or doing nothing. Ultimately if there is sustained concern about a person then the police may need to be asked to check on them, by forcing entry into the property if need be. As will be apparent from the instances cited in this book EDTs work frequently with the police and are used to consulting with them as to how to proceed in a variety of crisis situations. Other individuals and agencies, however, often do not have this familiar working relationship and might be reluctant or unwilling to contact the police about matters causing concern. One example of the difficulties that may ensue from this attitude concerned carers from an agency who had called on a man on several occasions one evening but had not been able to gain entry to him as they usually could. Just before midnight they telephoned the EDT worker on duty to tell him of their concerns for this man. The worker, who was literally on his way out of the door to attend to an urgent Mental Health Act assessment, suggested that the agency contact the police and ask them to investigate. The agency worker said they were not prepared to do this. The EDT worker left to attend to the assessment and made further inquiries about the man in question on his return to the office at 4.00 a.m. He found that the agency worker had not called the police and so did so himself. The police broke in to find the man lying on the floor, suffering from pneumonia. Fortunately, he survived but had he been there for much longer he might have died; had the agency contacted the police earlier instead of passing this responsibility on to the EDT worker who had much less knowledge of the man and his needs than they did he would not have suffered alone for as long as he had done.

Some people's reluctance to call the police is understandable. Embarrassment and expense can result from the police forcing entry to a property because the person living there does not answer the door when it later emerges that they had been invited out to Sunday lunch and had forgotten to inform the care agency of this. Conversely, as the case example above shows, a person's life may be at risk if appropriate and timely action is not taken when it needs to be. It is a notable and recurrent feature of EDT work that while individuals and agencies may think it reasonable to contact EDT about a legitimate concern or possible crisis they resist the idea of reporting that same concern to the police. They must, therefore, regard the two services quite differently. EDT workers often tell such callers that it is in the interests of the person they are calling about that they speak to the police directly about their concern, yet still they may be reluctant to do so.

One woman called, late at night, about a neighbour she had seen to be in a confused and distressed state unsuccessfully trying to gain entry to his accommodation. She was concerned about this man because she had seen him struggling to get into his property in this way for several nights previously. The EDT worker she spoke to suggested she contacted the police as they were best placed to visit immediately and assess the needs of such vulnerable adults. At this point the caller became indignant and abusive. She told the worker that social workers never *do* anything, they just sit on their backsides all day and worm their way out of their responsibilities. She had done her bit; it was up to the worker – if he wanted to leave the man to suffer, she was certainly going to do no more. The EDT worker did call the police who saw the request for their involvement as legitimate, visited and were able to assist. The EDT worker was left wondering why, given the well-motivated and clearly appropriate request for help, the caller had regarded it as acceptable to report her concerns to EDT but unacceptable to report them to the police.

Homelessness, financial problems and domestic violence

Because housing offices and benefits agencies are not open out of office hours EDT will often provide a gate-keeping/referral function for these services. Adults might have become vulnerable because they are homeless. This may be because they usually reside at an address which has become damaged by fire or flood (see also partnership working with emergency planning officers, Chapter 8) or because they have newly arrived in an area and are considered vulnerable because of mental disorder or disability. Partnership working with voluntary agencies which may be able to assist, such as the Red Cross, in the event of a fire can be helpful. Some EDTs have responsibility also to provide housing services out of normal office hours while others are supplied with rotas of housing officials who can be contacted and assess need themselves according to relevant criteria. Asylum seekers may also be referred to by EDTs although they have statutory responsibilities for juveniles rather than adults. Their responsibilities will be determined in the context of the role of the Home Office.

Women and children may be driven from their homes as a result of domestic violence (Aguilera, 1998). Even when they (part) own the house or they are named as the tenant, women may not feel sufficiently safe in the presence of violent men. Although they have the right to contact the police in such instances some women choose not to and prefer to leave their home. Domestic violence is a feature of many situations in which children are abused or at risk of abuse and this often has tragic consequences – 43 per cent of female murder victims are killed by partners or ex-partners (Cleaver et al., 1999: 30). Housing authorities often work in conjunction with local Women's Aid refuges to provide emergency accommodation for women and children in need of it. Refuges do not give out their address or telephone number to the public and are often contacted only through a trusted intermediary, working around the clock, such as The Samaritans.

People in receipt of state benefits may contact EDT to say they have no money for gas, electricity or food. Their benefit may have been stolen or lost or they may have encountered an unexpected financial crisis. Such calls cause greater concern if callers have dependent children or weather conditions are severe. EDT workers will usually pass these requests on to representatives of the Benefits Agency who provide a limited out-of-hours covering service. These workers make their own assessment of need, based on their knowledge of the service user, and can make crisis loans in circumstances when they determine these to be justified. In extreme cases, perhaps to avoid children coming into care, EDT workers may provide a food parcel or vouchers to be used in a local supermarket.

Recommendations for good practice when working with vulnerable adults

- Appropriate adults acting on behalf of vulnerable adults should be aware of the nature, extent and limitations of their role.
- Partnership working should resolve difficulties in returning vulnerable adults home when no one agency has clear responsibility for doing this.
- Apparently trivial concerns should be acknowledged to have the subjective importance accorded them by service users.
- EDTs should be advised by daytime workers about what specifically helps to calm and reassure individual distressed service users.
- Lists of approved contractors should be available for dealing with practical difficulties.
- Liaison forums with informal carers should be attended and difficulties acknowledged and shared.
- The potentially transforming importance of EDT workers listening carefully and showing attention in certain situations should be recognised.
- EDTs should be invited to professionals' meetings which discuss consistent management of particularly difficult service users.
- Private care providers should report concerns directly to the police and not always rely on EDT to do this.
- Effective liaison and working relationships with the police should be in place.
- Those in need of emergency housing and money and victims of domestic violence should be responded to appropriately.

Management

CHAPTER 5

Training: given and received

EDTs offer rich possibilities for enabling qualifying students to demonstrate necessary competence in a wide range of skills as previous chapters of this book show. In this chapter practice wisdom, gained from experience, is shared and later illustrated by the comments of two social work students reflecting on their placements at an EDT. Consideration is then given to the training needs of post-qualifying workers. The training needs of EDT workers are then discussed and suggestions made as to ways in which these may best be met. The values and difficulties of multi-agency training are acknowledged. The chapter ends with recommendations for good practice in relation to both the training that can be made available by EDT workers and that which they themselves need.

Providing placements for qualifying students

The richness and diversity of learning opportunities potentially available in an EDT setting are apparent from previous chapters. The majority of social work students undertaking placements have to choose a speciality from those available and therefore gain detailed knowledge concerning one aspect of daytime social work. They are unlikely to have had many opportunities to experience and understand how their particular speciality fits in with the bigger picture of health and social care. It is because their work remains necessarily generic and because of the wide range of agencies with whom they work in partnership (see Chapter 8) that EDTs can help students to gain a more comprehensive view of the wider aspects of health and social care than they would be able to achieve from any other placement. The EDT workforce in most areas is an ageing one and it is not uncommon for many EDT workers to have been working as qualified social workers for more than twenty years (Social Service's Inspectorate, 1999). Working with qualifying students can therefore be of value to EDTs as they bring with them new ideas, contemporary theories, practices and research findings, and constantly ask questions about fundamental aspects of the work. This repeated exposure to a *newcomer perspective* helps EDT workers to see their practice through new eyes and to question things which when they might, otherwise, have taken for granted.

Once training institutions and students know that an EDT is prepared to offer placements requests might be made from several sources to different people. It is therefore advisable to establish a clear system that is routinely followed whenever a student may want to inquire about the possibility of a placement. For example, the host university contacts the local social service's training officer who sends out relevant details concerning the prospective student to the EDT manager. The EDT manager assesses the application for its suitability and, if it seems acceptable and appropriate, passes it on to the next available practice teacher in the team. That practice teacher also considers the suitability of the request, and would then arrange to meet the student to discuss the possibility of working together. If all parties agree to this placement the necessary detailed arrangements can be made.

For EDTs where two or more people work together at times it is essential that all team members are in agreement to students being offered placements. This is because, although nominated practice teachers might plan to work as many shifts as possible alongside their student this will not always be possible for several reasons; the student's availability for work might not always correspond with the practice teacher's shift pattern, practice teachers will usually have some times of holiday or sick leave which requires another team member to deputise for them, another team member may be going on an interesting visit which could help the student demonstrate some necessary competence. They might then take the student out with them, deputising for the practice teacher in some aspects of the teaching role. In addition to being willing to do this these other team workers need a clear understanding of where their teaching role stops and the practice teacher's starts in relation to the student on placement. The careful handling of student placements and detailed management that this calls for, merits the team regularly making time at team meetings to discuss the needs of both students and team members in respect of the placement in the context of team functioning.

While EDT work offers frequent opportunities to learn about many aspects of crisis intervention it does not often allow students to demonstrate competence in areas such as planning and ongoing work. For this reason the practice teacher may need to negotiate some time for the student to work in a daytime team, as part of their placement, so that these competencies can be shown. It is sometimes debated whether EDT is better as a first or second placement. Does it provide a valuable introduction to the wider world of health and social care which can later be consolidated in a second placement? Alternatively, should a placement with EDT be offered only to experienced students who have some idea of what they might be dealing with and who have already some experience of statutory work? One EDT with experience of many student placements found that these issues were less significant as determinants of a successful outcome of a placement than the quality of psychological *hardiness* (Kobasa, 1982). This quality is not acquired as the result of age or experience but reflects a basic way of seeing the world, other people, and oneself. The 'hardy' person will generally be able to be open to the extremities and pain of crises without needing to minimise or deny these. They will have a resilient, 'bouncing back' quality which enables them not to be fazed or floored by the immediate and cumulative effects of what they are exposed to. They have a 'basic trust' (Erikson, 1951) in themselves and others which enables them to have hope for the future and enables them to see the crisis through to its optimum resolution. The potential for this capacity for psychological hardiness is the single most valuable attribute for EDT students and workers alike.

Kolb's (1984) model of adult learning styles is seen to be relevant in EDT settings. There are opportunities for those who prefer to learn by doing (*activists*) and who are keen to answer the telephone or go out on a visit. *Reflectors* can enjoy observing others at work, discussing calls after they have been responded to and considering visits after they have been completed. *Theorists* can discuss the role of theory in relation to the work with their practice teacher, while *pragmatists* can benefit from considering options for responding to future experiences and experimenting with different approaches when next called upon to act. Whilst all these styles are desirable within social work EDT students tend to be either primarily activists who may sometimes need restraining or reflectors who need encouragement to get directly involved more quickly and more often. Each calls for different responses from their practice teacher. If students first acknowledge their student status when answering the telephone then service users are not under the illusion that they are speaking to a qualified worker; and students need not then feel inadequate if they have to ask others for advice or refer the call to other team members.

The potential for intimacy that might develop between two people working closely together through difficult crisis situations at night should be acknowledged by both practice teacher and student as should the possibility of oppressive attitudes and abuse of power within the teaching/learning relationship (Thompson, 1993, 2002; Preston-Shoot, 1995; Dalrymple and Burke, 1998). The practice teacher should be supported by colleagues and be well-supervised so that they can share difficulties and celebrate successes. The carefully detailed selection process outlined above is of great importance when considering a student placement at EDT because, for the wrong student such a placement can be confusing, threatening, and de-skilling. For the right student, however, an EDT placement can be eye-opening, confidence building, and even exhilarating. This is shown by the two following quotations (taken from Smith et al., 1998) from erstwhile students reflecting upon their EDT placements:

> *For the first week I mainly observed, and began to acquaint myself with, office procedures and layout. I was able to see the tempo of the office change from peaceful and reflective work to periods of high activity at the ring of a 'phone bell. The expertise and skill of the team to field the calls in the right direction was amazing. I became acutely aware of the amount I knew nothing about and spent my days digesting Codes of Practice and roles of social workers and my evenings trying to make sense of office activities. My main concern was taking 'phone calls. I was unable to give the first class service that users needed and was fast becoming 'phone phobic! The team were very supportive and encouraging but the*

pressure of having to perform in front of the experts was overwhelming. Eventually I had to take the plunge when the office was in one of its frantically busy modes and it was necessary for me to act. The 'secrecy' button on the 'phone and the declaration of my student status at the outset enabled me to fumble my way to competency. The task has now become second nature. The experience I gained from participating in this expert team is invaluable.

My time with the team has been of great value in developing professional skills. I have been fortunate not only in receiving constant supervision from my own practice teacher, but (also) from the rest of the team. They have always been able to give me time and support, answering any questions that I may have. In a way it has been like having a team of my own practice teachers. The team work efficiently together, when prioritising work and deciding upon appropriate visits. Decisions are made effectively, and while under constant pressure, a team member is able to discuss best solutions with colleagues, giving me great insight into the importance of team work. By the nature of the work this is a highly stressful placement to be in and great concern was taken by the team to ensure that issues I was involved in were discussed and 'resolved' before I left the office. My college tutor remarked, 'I feel everyone should do a spell with EDT before qualifying' and I have to say, I agree with this. For any student wanting a good placement, this is a great opportunity and should be 'grabbed' without hesitation.

These two quotations illustrate several of the points made above. The first student (quoted) neatly encapsulates how quickly the tempo of EDT work can change, from being peaceful and reflective to a period of high activity at the ring of a telephone. She recognises the necessity for EDT workers to have a multi-faceted knowledge of the wider networks of which they are a part. She offers insight as to how repeatedly watching skilled and experienced practitioners at work can actually be disabling rather than empowering as she was made even more aware of her own relative lack of knowledge and skills. This aspect of a student's learning requires acknowledgement, encouragement, and careful handling by the practice teacher and other team members. Some students attempt to deal with a felt lack of experience by over-compensating and making out that they are more proficient than they actually are. Ultimately, this does not help the student, service users or the team but it is an understandable response to the 'pressure of having to perform in front of the experts'. Because students need to be more or less constantly observed and monitored by their practice teacher or deputy their responses as an EDT worker are nearly always public. There is no place to hide or opportunity to practice styles in private. At times, therefore, it is understandable that the student should experience an uncomfortable degree of pressure resulting from such constant surveillance.

The student's description of 'taking the plunge' at a busy time in the office is an example of a willingness to move out of Kolb's (1984) 'reflector' role and into that of 'activist' – learning by doing, rather than by watching others. She shows how, from an initial nervousness, she was helped to 'fumble her way to competency' by declaration of her student status. It is through navigating this appropriate transition from feeling overwhelmed and inadequate towards recognising that one has a relevant and useful role that sound adult learning and successful outcome from EDT placements are accomplished. Practice teachers who encourage those initially nervous students to come to recognise that they do have valuable skills and abilities, in some ways have an easier task than those working with students who believe themselves to be more capable than they actually are and who need to learn and accept this.

The second student quoted highlights the importance of necessarily having the whole team involved in practice teaching, 'In a way it has been like having a team of my own practice teachers'. Students on placement will often comment on the differing individual styles of team members who all work nevertheless to common aims and standards. Seeing that a range of responses to a similar problem may be equally appropriate and effective can provide a valuable learning experience for the student and one which empowers them to develop their own style. The student (quoted) also notes ways in which team members will 'look out for' and support one another, and clearly appreciates the value of the de-brief after a shift ends so that work is not 'taken home' in an unhelpful way. She concludes by supporting her tutor's view that all daytime workers would gain an enhanced understanding of the social work process were they to spend some time with EDT.

Some EDT workers with a particular interest in practice teaching have formed part of a panel interviewing prospective students for places on qualifying social work courses. This is another way in which others can be reminded of the relevance and importance of the EDT role and of the fact that social work tasks are undertaken outside, as well as inside, normal office hours.

Although this discussion has concentrated on students qualifying to be social workers, others training in health and social care fields can also gain from spending some time with EDTs to see what they do and how they do it. Student nurses, police officers and doctors have found it useful to experience EDT perspectives and to see for themselves the wide-ranging aspects of the work and how situations are responded to. With the current emphasis on 'continuous professional development' (Thompson, 2002) qualified and established workers in health and social care settings are also encouraged to learn from EDTs about their work.

Providing opportunities for students undertaking post-qualifying training

Relationships between EDTs and daytime teams or partner agencies can be improved by each seeing the reality of working conditions and experiences of the other. EDT workers will perform liaison roles, visiting other teams and discussing issues of mutual importance. Sometimes they will engage in daytime Approved Social Work (ASW) or child protection duty to experience the reality of daytime services and draw lessons relevant to optimal EDT functioning. EDT workers may go out with police officers on shifts for similar reasons. Conversely, daytime workers, from the UK and abroad, have accompanied EDT workers on their shifts, and thereby gained enhanced understanding. The potential for using such useful learning to mutual benefit is not always realised, however. It is easier (and sometimes more immediately satisfying) to be critical of and negative about what other services do or do not do when responding to crises rather than to go and find out more about the reality of the conditions and circumstances in which they work. If, however, time can be made available away from the crisis setting, where prejudices and inadequacies can sometimes be recognised, shared, and discussed improved joint working results.

One consequence of professionals now being required to demonstrate continuous professional development is that several post-qualifying training courses are available and attendance required for some aspects of working roles. Anyone wishing to work as an ASW under the 1983 Mental Health Act needs successfully to complete a 60 day post-qualifying training. In 2001 the post-qualifying award in child care was introduced, the intention being that all social workers working directly with children would gain this award, which currently takes one year of part-time study. (Other post-qualifying and advanced awards in social work are also available.) Supervisors, mentors or assessors are needed for all of these various awards and many experienced EDT workers are well placed to perform this role. Placements at EDT will illustrate common dilemmas in crisis work, particularly in child protection and mental health work and can, at the same time, facilitate valuable networking and enhanced understanding between daytime and night-time services.

As well as offering useful training experiences to others EDT workers themselves also need to use other opportunities available for their own professional development. These needs are now considered.

Training needs of EDT workers

It is apparent from previous chapters that EDT workers need to keep up to date with changes in legislation and codes of practice which are central to their work. In particular, relevant knowledge of the Mental Health Act 1983, the Police and Criminal Evidence Act 1984, and the Children Act 1989 are crucial. While EDT workers need to know the aspects of this legislation which apply to their work, they do not need to know it in its entirety. Rather, they need to know its application to their own frequently encountered crisis situations and will, therefore, often refer repeatedly to the same few sections of legislation. Because of this specific focus their training needs are well-defined. Most training arranged for daytime workers will include consideration of many wider aspects of health and social care work which are largely irrelevant to the EDT role. The value of attending training events arranged for daytime workers (such as 'academic', rather than directly relevant, interest, the awareness of the 'bigger picture' and opportunities for networking), has to be balanced against the specialist needs of EDT workers for training with particular relevance to their role and duties.

Some attendance at daytime training events is compulsory. For example, it is a condition of continuing to be warranted as an ASW that workers attend a minimum number of training days each year. EDT workers also need to keep up to date with essential aspects of child protection work and changes in the organisation of daytime structures which affect how services are delivered, such as the relatively recent creation of youth offending teams. Fearing their particular and specific needs for training might be overlooked in a context where daytime perspectives predominate, EDTs have joined together, across geographical boundaries, to establish training forums where EDT concerns are addressed particularly from an EDT perspective.

EDT training forums have existed in the North of England for some years and have more recently been developed in the Midlands and South of the country (Smith, 1999a). The more recent of these forums have coincided with, or grown out of, the formation of the Emergency Social Services Association (ESSA) in 1997 which currently has a membership of 104 EDTs across the United Kingdom. The ESSA structure of regional groups provides a context where training can be planned and evaluated while bi-annual conferences provide opportunities for further training, networking, and discussion of matters of importance. It is a refreshing change for EDT workers to attend training tailored to their needs, and to be with others who see the world from the same perspective and speak the same language, acknowledging the same issues to be of importance. Similar basic conditions and working environments can already be assumed and there is no need to explain first principles from the beginning, something which commonly happens in more daytime orientated training environments.

EDT training forum days have included days on:

- Promoting safe working practices.
- Child care legal updates.
- Considering the *Open all hours?* report in detail.
- Using actors to bring to life issues in complex interview situations.
- Comparing basic staffing structures, conditions of service and ways of working.
- Forensic aspects of EDT work.
- Customer satisfaction surveys, performance indicators and managing change.
- Lessons for EDTs from reviews of child deaths.
- Discussing key aspects of mental health work.

Sometimes an expert speaker from 'outside' the EDT framework has been invited to the group to stimulate discussion. On other occasions EDT workers themselves have provided the input and led the day's programme. As well as creating a useful opportunity to hear about and debate the subject under discussion, these training days also offer EDT workers a valuable opportunity for networking that they are not able to get from within their own borough/county. Training also offers workers opportunities to be proactive and thereby influence what the future may bring, rather than passively sit back and wait for prevailing changes to shape essential services.

Because, by nature, EDT work is essentially reactive, workers on shift have few opportunities to be proactive, and to think about decisions in detail before making them. Now, however, all out of hours services are facing quite different demands and expectations from those encountered several years ago. This is mainly because of the nature and degree of social change which has occurred recently. If EDTs do not want simply to get dragged along in the wake of the latest fashionable notion they need to be proactive – to see what influence they do have and exploit this to the full (Covey, 1992). Whenever a significant ideological change impacts on an EDT training day (either provided internally, just for the team, or held in the company of others in a training forum), this can be an effective way of hearing and exchanging views about the matter. Such days make space for objections to be voiced, considered and allowed their place in influencing whatever is finally decided upon. As EDT workers work mostly alone, unless they can see the value of working in proposed new ways to take account of new thinking and initiatives, they are likely not to be willing to do so. Getting them 'on board' is crucial. Examples of topics which have been considered on EDT training days are: writing a business plan at a time of departmental reorganisation, devising and implementing a system of ethnic monitoring and debating how to incorporate performance indicators into EDT work. These training days have led to more willing, co-operative and successful implementation of agreed systems.

EDT workers may have little or no time in which to reflect upon decisions made after a particular event if a new crisis quickly intervenes and demands immediate attention. Planning for, and participating in training, clears a space in which to reflect on significant events and to learn from experience. In Cell's terms (1984: viii) training can bring secondary reflection to primary thinking:

> As we are transacting with our world our minds are continually at work interpreting these transactions and the situations in which we enact them. This is primary thinking. It is the spontaneous and usually habitual activity that forms the background of our actions and reactions . . . Primary thinking is often laced with bias, prejudice, superstition, fanaticism, provincialism, exaggeration and the like. Through secondary reflection we may challenge and work toward overcoming these distortions. If we learn to carry the results with us and to apply them deliberately as we renew our transactions with our world, we gradually transform our primary thinking . . . It may also happen that in our primary thinking we sow the seeds of greater clarity, of enrichment, or of alternatives in our ways of seeing and understanding. Secondary reflection helps to bring these beginnings to fruition and to clear the way for further beginnings.

The importance and potential value of reflective practice is currently emphasised in health and social care (Taylor, 1996, 2000; Thompson, 2002). One of the advantages of Cell's description of the ways in which secondary reflection can transform primary thinking is that he acknowledges the latter to be laced with, 'bias, prejudice, superstition, fanaticism, provincialism, exaggeration . . .'. These are among the constituents of oppressive thinking and practice. Cell contends that we may not be able to prevent such thoughts from being initially part of consciousness. Nevertheless, they do not need to remain in consciousness if subjected to and transformed by secondary reflection. Secondary reflection therefore transforms primary thinking so that practice moves towards becoming anti-oppressive rather than oppressive (Issitt, 1999).

Multi-agency training

Thus far this discussion has concentrated upon EDTs training and being trained within a single agency. Over recent years, however, a trend towards multi-agency training has developed and 'training pools' comprising trainers from various agencies have become commonplace in both adult's and children's services. Community mental health teams are staffed by professionals from different orientations such as nursing, social work and occupational therapy, who have undergone different primary trainings. When colleagues join together on training days course content is planned with this in mind. Much child protection training is also provided in a multi-agency context with health visitors, social workers, nurses, police officers, teachers, education welfare officers and other statutory and voluntary workers coming together in one setting to learn, together.

When multi-agency training works well different professionals can talk together, share their varying perspectives and experiences and see how their particular contribution fits into the overall, broader picture. It is often more difficult to blame and judge people when they are encountered face-to-face. As people are seen to be human, they are demonised less easily. Useful contacts can be established, so when people later work together on a case this is likely to be made easier by the fact they have met and talked previously.

Such training is not, however, always useful and productive. The fact that someone has chosen to work in a particular role in health and social care and not a different one means there is something about *that* role (and its associated ways of seeing oneself, the world and others) which appeals more than a similar role. Such important aspects of differential motivation are not easily forgotten or traded and, when it goes wrong, multi-agency training can act as a catalyst for highlighting differences and divisions between workers. Some may use the training day to express their discontent (and perceived righteousness) publicly and repeatedly to shame others. The consequence of this can be people leaving the training even more confirmed in their stereotyping and disdain of others and more convinced that others have got it wrong whereas they have got it right.

Two professional groups with whom EDTs often work closely are police custody sergeants and doctors especially approved under section 12 of the Mental Health Act. Joint training with both of these groups has proved useful. It is particularly difficult for doctors and police officers to be available to attend training events because of the many demands on their time. Even if agreement is given to attend when the training is being planned, a crisis, sickness, or need to provide cover for a colleague at short notice often disrupts the plan and the joint training does not take place. Individuals within organisations can be keen to support training initiatives but then move elsewhere too quickly for their hopes to be realised. Despite such difficulties, it can be worthwhile to persevere.

A training event was planned and delivered jointly by a psychiatrist and ASW that formed part of the training of general practitioners with a special interest in mental health work and who wanted to become approved under section 12 of the Mental Health Act. Discussion and use of role play highlighted common dilemmas and the contacts and relationships formed on the training day proved helpful later when doctors and ASWs were working together.

One EDT arranged a number of training events with police custody sergeants. These events created a forum wherein different perspectives could be shared in relation to the mutual difficulties commonly encountered. Social workers and police officers are assigned different and complementary roles in child protection, mental health work, and work with vulnerable adults (see previous chapters for examples). They need one another to work professionally to agreed protocols and within necessary timescales. When this is successfully achieved, and the pieces fit neatly together as legislation intended, the outcomes are satisfying and beneficial because each partner recognises that they have achieved more by working together than either could have done on their own. When mistakes, delays and misunderstandings predominate, the ensuing acrimony can last for years especially when allegations of incompetence and stories of inefficiency are circulated, gaining potency with each telling, and pass into folklore. Successful joint training helps to address such matters. It can work both proactively, allowing services to plan together for ideal responses to crises yet to arise, and retrospectively, as contentious episodes can be deconstructed and learned from.

Good joint training can also lead to mutually acceptable agreements about procedural matters. A local police service, understanding the EDTs staffing levels and constraints, had agreed that, apart from rare instances, such as when potential forensic evidence may need immediate attention, they would not ask EDT workers to act as appropriate adults in interviews after midnight. Following a useful joint training exercise, in which the EDT was made more aware of the police officers' perspectives, they agreed to modify their position of always insisting on a solicitor's *presence* in interviews conducted under the Police and Criminal Evidence Act 1984. The training event enabled them to see that, in some circumstances, consultation with a solicitor might suffice. While none of those involved in the training were of a sufficient level of authority to actually write policy concerning these issues they decided that since they were the people involved in *doing* the work they could stipulate and adhere to what they believed to be appropriate and manageable working practices. These practices have since gained such widespread recognition and acceptance, and been passed down to people newly in post, that they have assumed the status of being the most carefully-followed policies.

The chapter now concludes with recommendations for good practice in training given and received by EDT workers.

Recommendations for good practice in training

EDTs as providers of training:

- EDTs should include practice teachers as they have much to offer and to gain from having students on placement.
- There should be a clear, straightforward and workable system whereby requests for placements are considered and decided upon.
- The whole team should be in agreement with any placement, and support both students on placements and the practice teacher.
- Links should be made with daytime teams to enable students to achieve and demonstrate necessary competencies.
- The particular needs of both *activist* and *reflector* students should be acknowledged and worked with.
- Anti-oppressive practice and practice teaching should be promoted.

EDTs as recipients of training:

- Some training will be undertaken with daytime teams so that EDT workers can update knowledge and practices and network with others.
- Training forums should be established so that particular needs of EDT workers can be considered from an EDT perspective.
- Training should take account of the dual needs to be both proactive and reflective.
- The advantages and disadvantages of multi-agency training should be recognised.

CHAPTER 6

Health and safety issues: assessing risks

This chapter discusses the various risks inherent in EDT work. Having outlined principle underpinning risk assessment it goes on to consider ways in which EDT workers may be at ris as a result of the sleep deprivation that is a consequence of the long shifts they work at a stretch Their personal safety and sense of well-being may be at risk from disturbed, threatening an potentially violent service users. EDT workers are also frequently responding to the needs c service users who may represent a danger to themselves or others. They therefore need to mak concise and comprehensive assessments of complex situations often based on little informatio and with little time to do so (Clifford and Williams, 2002). The chapter concludes with som cautions about becoming overly dependent on risk assessment tools and some recommendation for good practice in relation to risk assessment in an EDT context.

Principles underpinning risk assessment

Section 2 of The Health and Safety at Work Act 1974 gives every employer the duty, '. . . t ensure, so far as is reasonably practicable the health, safety and welfare at work of all hi employees'. Section 7 (a) gives every employee the duty to 'take reasonable care for the healt and safety of themselves and others who may be affected by their acts or omissions' and 7 (t to, 'co-operate with their employer or any other person to enable legal obligations to be met Over recent years the duties of employer and employee have increasingly entailed the completio of risk assessments.

Risk assessments should be carried out whenever any threat or danger could be reasonabl foreseen to pose a harmful consequence of any action or omission of an employee. Employer will therefore require employees to complete a risk assessment regarding their use of displa screen equipment, since this represents a potential threat to the health and safety of the employe in their place of work. Electrical equipment and precautions in the event of a fire should b routinely tested. Employees should complete risk assessments before and while visiting potentiall violent service users. Employers should provide workable policies and establish safe practic guidelines as well as pro-formas for completion of risk assessments and a system for reportin incidents in the event of something going wrong. Such reporting will ideally highlight areas of need and difficulty and give employers an opportunity to respond to identified gaps in safe working practices.

When taking possible risks into account it can be helpful to do this literally and take them into account. Words are notorious for having shades of meaning that elude precise definition and the same word can mean different things to different people at different times. Numbers are more precise and it is useful to think of risks as percentages or as being scored on a scale as well as using words to describe them. The two most important questions regarding risks in health and social care are:

1. How likely is it that the service user will do X?
2. If they do X how bad (significant) will it be?

The two principal criteria for describing risk therefore are likeliness and significance and these can be seen as two axes on a graph. For example, a service user threatening self harm may be thought to be quite likely to carry out this threat (8/10) but to do so in a fairly minor way (3/10). The anticipated likelihood of risk is therefore thought to be high but the expected significance relatively low. The risk calculated is therefore lower than for someone who scores 8/10 on both dimensions and higher than someone who scores 4/10 for likelihood and 2/10 for significance. By taking the anticipated risk into account in this way people can be categorised as low, medium, or high risk. Workers are likely to act in response to high risk, leave alone in response to low risk and seek further information/think and discuss the situation further in response to medium risk.

The 1974 Health and Safety at Work Act was drawn up principally with risks arising from conditions of work in factories and the safe handling of machinery in mind. Over recent years, however, there has been an increasing emphasis on psychological aspects of health and safety at work. The Health and Safety Executive have been visiting acute psychiatric admission wards and residential children's homes to interview the staff there and become aware of the challenges they face from day-to-day, night-to-night.

In the groundbreaking case of Walker v Northumberland County Council (1995) the High Court ruled that Walker's employers had been negligent in the duty of care owed to him. Walker was a child protection manager in a social services department. He suffered a breakdown at work as a consequence of too-heavy a workload. After some time on sick leave, he returned to work having been promised additional support and resources. Neither was forthcoming and Walker suffered a second breakdown. His employers were found liable for the second breakdown on the grounds that it was foreseeable in the light of the first. This court case established two important principles: firstly, that stress in social work is intrinsic, and secondly, that it is foreseeable. Employers owe a duty of care to their employees and should take these two characteristics into account when assessing what constitutes a healthy and safe working environment. Although the Walker case concerned issues arising from work in a social services department, th principles considered and resulting judgement have relevance to many other health and soci care workers.

An assessment of health and safety at work needs to include consideration of the advers effects of words upon workers, as well as actions. Policies addressing violence and aggression i the workplace, and racial incidents, will typically include words and actions as being potentiall offensive and unacceptable. Having supervised many experienced and competent workers ove the years, it seems to me that service users' words, rather than their actions, have stayed wit and hurt these workers more deeply and more often. Sometimes graphically detailed obscen messages or threats can be left on EDT ansaphones which cause understandable distress to th worker needing to play them back

When acting as an appropriate adult in an interview conducted by the police one femal EDT worker heard precise and intricate details over several hours describing how a young mal had tortured his girlfriend to death. When in this type of situation the worker's imagination tend to 'fill in' the details of what they are hearing and this can be profoundly disturbing (Smith ar Nurtsen, 1998). The fact that the 'appropriate adult' who sat in on the police interviews with th notorious killer, Fred West, later sued because of what she was made to *hear* is a furthe indication of the need to attend to mental, as well as physical, health and safety needs. Notice are appearing with increasing frequency in public services offices warning that abusive languag or actions directed at staff working there will not be tolerated and that the police will be called necessary. It is an unfortunate sign of our times that police officers are routinely in attendance ε some accident and emergency departments in hospitals because of violence towards the medic staff, and that security guards attend reception areas of council offices.

Writing of the important but elusive nature of risk assessment Carson (1996: 4) warns that

> . . . *even though it is so central to the law, 'risk' is not a discrete legal concept. There ∗ no 'law of risk or risk taking'. The key legal concepts are 'negligence' and 'recklessness'. . The key issue, in practice, is whether the person, for example a social worker, acted in manner comparable to how others would have acted.*

He goes on (1996: 5) to say that however diligent practitioners try to be in completing ris assessments the law provides no certainty in this area, '. . . the law, at best, provides checklist procedures and frameworks. It provides a foundation for professionals to work within and to utiliz to justify their risks; it rarely provides direct answers'. The concept of negligence is of particula importance to those working in the caring professions as in order to be liable for negligence th person being sued must owe a duty of care to the person injured. The duty of care is the definin principle of relationships between those employed in health and social care services and thos they work with. Carson argues (1996: 9) that although there can be a tendency to perceive ris as 'inherently evil' a preferable view is to define risk taking, '. . . in terms of comparing an balancing likely benefits with likely harms'. For all of its current popularity, risk assessment remains, like all attempts to predict the future, an inexact science.

Nonetheless, the Health and Safety Executive (1998) propose five steps to risk assessment:

- Look for the hazards.
- Decide who might be harmed and how.
- Evaluate the risks. Are existing precautions adequate or should more be done?
- Record findings.
- Review your assessment and revise it as necessary.

Recording thoughts of possible/likely risk before making a visit, or deciding not to follow up on a telephone call, are particularly important as they offer the worker some protection against a later charge of negligence, should things subsequently go wrong. Workers in health and social care cannot reasonably be expected to predict the future so accurately as to keep all people completely free from danger to themselves and/or others in every situation (although the tone of some inquiries after the event may suggest otherwise!). However, service users have a right to expect a reasonable duty of care from those professionally involved with them. A risk assessment completed before finalising a decision to act or not to act showing why and how a decision was arrived at (and why a different decision was not reached) is proof of the worker having thought things through, hopefully agreed the decision with others, and weighed up what seemed to them at the time to be the balance of probabilities. This goes some way toward countering a charge of negligence. Because of the long hours they work at a stretch one possible risk often posed to EDT workers is how lack of sleep may affect their judgement.

Working long hours and driving-related risks

As explained in Chapter 1, most EDTs include an overnight shift in their rota. This could be of between fifteen and a half hours, for example, from 6 p.m.–9.30 a.m. or twelve hours in between 8 p.m. and 8 a.m. Some EDTs may leave gaps in their cover at times of least demand such as after 2 a.m. but these are in the minority as most social services departments like to have at least one representative available 24 hours a day. One of the recommendations of the inquiry into the care and treatment of Christopher Clunis, who murdered a man whilst receiving psychiatric care in the community, (Ritchie et al., 1994) was that a social worker approved under the Mental Health Act 1983 would be available at all times. This provides a further reason for ensuring a 24-hour availability of a suitably approved social worker.

It is to the financial advantage of EDT workers that they are contracted to work 'waking duty' shifts for which they are paid an hourly rate. If they were contractually allowed to sleep unless their response is required, it could be argued that they should not be paid for each hour spent on duty but would be employed on a 'standby' or 'sleeping in' basis for which they would only be paid for hours actually spent working. Most EDT workers like the overnight shift as it enables them to fulfil their contractual obligations for the week in relatively few sessions. For example, a worker who is on duty for two overnight shifts of 15 hours each and one weekend day shift of eight hours has completed their week's work in three shifts leaving the rest of the week at their disposal. For established EDT workers, this way of structuring time becomes a way of life which opens up possibilities for the rest of the week. Some EDT workers have child care responsibilities which they can fulfil by working in EDT but could not fulfil if working 9 a.m.–5 p.m. Monday to Friday. Some have time consuming hobbies and interests, some do other jobs in the vacant hours.

Some EDT workers have wanted to extend their continuous hours of work beyond an overnight shift by working beyond this shift and into the next working day making a 24-hour long shift. In the past some workers have lived many miles away from the EDT base and would arrive for the weekend on a Friday night, work as many shifts as possible, and return home to live an EDT work-free life for the rest of the week. The European Working Time Directive (1998) has provided further reasons for examining the effects on staff and their performance of long working hours. Some EDTs have shortened or eliminated the long overnight shift in order to conform with this directive.

The European Working Time Directive was introduced primarily to provide employees who were previously expected to work long hours at a time some legal protection from being compelled to do so. It caused employers to think carefully about the duration of shifts their staff are expected to work and to justify any exceptions to the limits laid down. Recent studies of and research into the effects of sleep deprivation have pointed to the dangers arising when people have had insufficient sleep (Rajaratnam and Arendt, 2001). Martin (2002: 6) claims that, '. . . sleepiness is responsible for far more deaths on the roads than alcohol or drugs'. He cites examples (2002: 33–4) of a driver of a pickup truck who veered off the road after apparently falling asleep at the wheel in California in 1994, 12 passengers died as a result. In 1995 a bus driver in France seemed to fall asleep and lost control of his bus. The resulting accident caused 22 deaths and 32 injuries. In the United Kingdom in 2001 Gary Hart fell asleep whilst driving near Selby and his vehicle subsequently crashed onto a railway line causing the deaths of ten train passengers. Hart admitted having had no sleep the night before the crash but, despite this, considered himself to be capable of driving safely.

Martin (2002: 51, 63, 65–6) claims that working at night causes people to offend basic principles of health and well-being and that driving while deprived of sleep can be just as dangerous and undesirable as driving under the influence of alcohol:

Working at night forces people to perform at a time when their biological clocks are telling them to sleep, and to sleep when their biological clocks are telling them they should be awake. They perform worse when they are at work, and they are less able to sleep when they go home, as a result of which they become tired and accident-prone . . . In a more sleep-conscious world it would no longer be socially acceptable, let alone admirable, for people to drive or turn up for work suffering from severe fatigue, any more than it is now acceptable to be drunk in the workplace or behind the wheel of a car . . . Tired people tend to persist with their current activity regardless of whether it is appropriate . . . (they) resemble drunk people in several respects. Most obviously, tiredness and alcohol both hamper our ability to perform tasks that require judgement, attention, quick reactions and co-ordination . . . Tired people, like drunk people, have a misplaced confidence in their own abilities . . . So next time you miss a night's sleep, try to remember that your driving ability will be as bad as if you had a blood-alcohol level that would be illegal in most countries.

Bearing in mind the far-reaching consequences that can result from decisions made by EDT workers, sometimes when extremely tired, this is a warning that should be heeded. Like many sensible warnings, however, it is easier to acknowledge the sensible advice offered than to change behaviours as a result of it. EDT workers often pride themselves on being able to 'cope with anything', often alone, and his has led to accusations of a 'macho' culture in which workers are blind to and/or disregarding of the true level of risk inherent in situations. The job can become addictive for people working repeatedly long shifts; their life becomes dominated by the work, their body clocks and timescales out of phase with those of significant others, and the sleep-deprived adrenalin highs become the most affirming aspect of their lives. This is a common finding among those who work in extreme crisis situations (Hodgkinson and Stewart, 1991).

Other driving-related risks for EDT workers may be posed if the worker is either asked to, or decides to, transport service users. The police may ask a worker to transport a service user home after an interview or an EDT worker may decide to take a service user to hospital to avoid a long wait for an ambulance. Sometimes workers may decide to transport service users because they have met them on several occasions previously and think that they know them. Generally, this is unlikely to happen and should be avoided whenever possible. Taxis or professional escorting services should be employed instead. As with all aspects of EDT work, however, it is impossible to predict every eventuality and there are exceptions to most rules.

Nevertheless the potential dangers in a situation where workers believe they know service users and are therefore safe with them, merit special mention. One EDT worker drove some 50 miles at 2 a.m. to collect a young person in care and to return him to the area from which he came. He had completed a risk assessment, based on what was known, and concluded that it was safe for him to do so. The young person was returned home safely and without incident. Several days later however, the same young person was arrested for stabbing the eye of a member of the public. It emerged that he had been experiencing paranoid delusions for some weeks, and perceived others as being a threat to him. He also later revealed that he had entertained these paranoid thoughts about the EDT worker while being driven home by him. This case provides a reminder that for all we think we know about people and situations there is always more that we don't know and we need to allow for this not-knowing when assessing risks.

A common risk posed for those working in health and social care generally and for EDT workers in particular is that of working with those who are, or may become, a danger to themselves or others. These risks are now considered.

Working with people who are, or may become, a danger to themselves or others

Dealing with people who are, or may become, a danger to themselves and/or others is a constant feature of working with service users with mental health problems (see Chapter 3). It is important that social workers approved under The Mental Health Act 1983 are seen not to act, 'in bad faith or without reasonable care' or, conversely, to act in good faith and without negligence (section 139, Mental Health Act). Part of not being negligent entails conducting a risk assessment which takes account of known or anticipated risks that may result from involvement (or lack of it) with service users.

Working with people who are known to have a history of self-harm is fraught with difficulties. Such people may call EDT saying they have taken a large overdose just prior to making the call or that they have just cut themselves or are cutting themselves while speaking. These calls present a dilemma to the worker. Will *just* listening be an adequate response or does action need to be taken? It is advisable for workers to share the decision to be made with appropriate others working at the same time, usually the police or covering general practitioner or psychiatrist. If they do this they have shown themselves not to be negligent in as much that they have alerted others to the possible risks involved and shared the decision making. Two or three different perspectives are nearly always preferable to one and contribute to a wider consideration of the matter needing attention. Sometimes EDT workers will decide that someone can be safely left whilst at other times decide that action should be taken. As the police will not always have officers available to respond to crisis calls of this kind the ambulance service may be contacted. Whilst on some occasions they may arrive to find someone in need of urgent medical attention, on others they may find the caller safe, well and unharmed (and possibly peacefully asleep!). Self-harming callers should not be disbelieved on the grounds that they are probably 'crying wolf'. Those involved in their care recognise that there may well not be a real need to respond to but feel a duty and obligation to respond to the possibility none-the-less.

While the completion of a risk assessment might aid decision making, in these cases such assessments can detail only anticipated probabilities and cannot be depended upon to guarantee desired outcomes. One EDT dealt with two service users who called to talk of harming themselves on most nights, and sometimes several times a night. Both repeatedly self-harmed, usually in relatively minor ways and were well known to ambulance and police services and their local hospitals. Repeated risk assessments by different EDT workers suggested that one of these young women was much more likely to kill herself than the other – she seemed more deeply disturbed, her self-harming attempts were more serious and she seemed to contend with deeper, more potent negative thoughts than the other. All EDT members were therefore shocked when they learned that the young woman thought less likely to kill herself had actually done so. Although she was subsequently believed to have died as the result of an attempt at suicide which went wrong rather than a genuine desire to be dead, it was a salutary reminder that for all we think we know there is much more that we do not know. One should never be totally confident of any risk assessment however well informed or shared.

EDTs will try to refer callers who essentially want only to talk about themselves and their problems, and who do not appear to meet the social service eligibility criteria, to telephone support lines set up for this purpose such as The Samaritans and Saneline (see Chapter 8). Nevertheless, service users are often discriminating about which service they choose to telephone, when, and with what hoped for response in mind. Several service users have said that they prefer to speak to a member of EDT because they are more likely to be engaged in conversation than they would be if they called The Samaritans who (intentionally) 'just listen' (see Chapter 9 for more details of service users' comments on EDTs).

Social workers also frequently work closely with people thought to be a potential danger to others. These may be adults believed to be at risk of abusing children in their care (see Chapter 2) or of being violent to other adults. Such a danger to others may be because of an underlying mental health problem but sometimes not. Situations of domestic violence can be particularly difficult to deal with as they can involve interrelated mental health issues, heavy drinking and/or drug abuse, child abuse and an apparently preferred tendency towards using violence as a means of communication. Again, risk assessments along with policies that make it clear when private confidentiality ends and public protection begins, are necessary. This is particularly important for effective partnership working. Chapter 3 provides examples of EDT work with people who have represented a danger to others as a result of mental health problems and Chapter 4 considers the role of appropriate adult under The Police and Criminal Evidence Act 1984 when workers have sat in on interviews of people suspected of murder. Those found guilty of and charged with this offence have been the ultimate danger to others and, unfortunately, they were not prevented from making their murderous fantasies a reality. When working with those known to be, or suspected of being, a danger to others, as well being concerned for the well being of these others, EDT workers also need to be mindful of their personal safety.

Personal safety issues

It is a tragedy of recent times that social workers have been killed while undertaking their duties (Norris, 1990). Often these workers have been killed by service users known to them and with whom they had thought they enjoyed a good relationship. It is a recurring criticism of social workers that, motivated by a desire to see the best in people, they are often unaware of the extent to which people can be hateful, destructive or murderous. This tendency to want to see and believe the best of others has been called 'the rule of optimism' (London Borough of Brent, 1985). Risk assessment calls for a cool, detached look at the potential for violence of which service users are capable, that should be balanced against the rule of optimism. All people can be seen as falling into one of two categories regarding risk: high risk, or risk not yet known. This way of seeing the potential for violence in all of us, given the wrong combination of circumstances and the wrong trigger factors, helps workers to maintain vigilance for possible risk and danger that ultimately may help to promote safer working practices.

Before visiting a service user, EDT workers should complete a risk assessment that identifies the potential hazards inherent in a situation and the supports available that help to balance these hazards. Most EDTs are currently insufficiently staffed to allow for two workers to visit service users together, although the kind of situation they are typically called out to, for example a mental health assessment on a mother when children are also involved, would often benefit from two people working together. While other professionals, usually the police or doctors, are likely to be involved in much child protection and mental health work at various stages, they are not dependably or continuously present throughout the entire process. A particularly vulnerable time for an approved social worker in the community can be when waiting for an ambulance to transport a service user who has been 'sectioned' and the doctors involved have completed their medical recommendations and left. The worker then needs to balance their legal duties and obligations to the service user, and others in close proximity, with the need to ensure their own safety. If the situation is perceived as being too dangerous for the worker to stay there alone, they should consider leaving and calling the police for assistance.

The clothing worn by social workers also has a bearing upon their personal safety. Most people will have at least some respect for a 'uniform' and respond differently to a police officer or ambulance worker in uniform than towards a social worker in 'ordinary' clothes. Putting on the uniform before a shift begins and taking it off again at the end may also afford those in the emergency services some psychological protection. They are more obviously dressing up for a performance of a role than social workers and de-roleing, when changing out of these clothes at the end of their shift (performance) (see Goffman, 1957). These actions can help create some symbolic distance between the individual and the job they do; this is psychologically healthy.

It is important that risk assessments of someone's potential dangerousness do not over-emphasise the security of certain places. At first sight it may appear that an assessment in the community entails greater risks than one in a police station when someone is in 'a place of safety'. However, some professionals have been more seriously assaulted when interviewing service users in police stations than they have in the community. It may be that people feel more vulnerable (and therefore more inclined to attack others) when not on their 'home territory' and, for some, the environment of and atmosphere in a police station may seem bewildering, frightening and oppressive.

When social workers in daytime teams make visits to service users thought to be potentially difficult, they are encouraged to let someone back at base know where they have gone and how long they expect to be. These visits may be recorded in a 'movements' book or made known to others, such as receptionists, working at the base. As most EDTs operate for much of the time with only one worker on duty there is often no colleague to tell of potentially difficult visits or to read a 'movements' book. There is therefore the need for an appropriate lone working policy and to have some kind of back up system, provided either internally by other team members or externally by a contracted provider, which charts a worker's progress and confirms their safe return. While inspections by The Health and Safety Executive, along with greater emphasis of appropriate risk assessments, have led to more carefully considered and arguably safer working practices over recent years, there is a danger in thinking that risk assessments provide 'the answer' to possible dangers inherent in the work. They do not.

Limitations of risk assessments

EDTs will often be working with people about whom they know very little. Someone may just have arrived in the area for the first time and need an assessment. They may apparently have no memory, not speak English or deliberately withhold true information about themselves. For EDTs covering ports and airports this is a particularly significant issue. While teams will have some access to daytime data bases which hold information on known service users this access is often partial at best, and computer systems cannot be depended upon to always be fully updated (Department of Health, 1999a). Given how little is sometimes known about service users one may wonder about the extent to which any risk assessment can be meaningfully completed other than to acknowledge that anyone can be potentially dangerous given the relevant combination of circumstances and trigger factors. Conversely, just as lack of information and previous knowledge may result in people being regarded as high risk, it is also true that the more information that is available with regard to a potential risk event the more it will be regarded as likely to happen (Kemshall and Pritchard, 1996/1997).

Beckett (2002: 10-1) argues that the idea of risk assessment has gained a reputation for precision which it does not deserve:

Behind the preoccupation with assessment in family social work is the idea that if we gather enough information, we ought to be able to rank families in order of risk and identify which are the really dangerous ones, which are the ones that are not acutely dangerous but do need help, and which are the ones that can be left to sort themselves out. In practice, this isn't quite so easy as it sounds. How do you translate the messy, complex, multidimensional, qualitative material you gather together in an assessment into an accurate, unidimensional and objective measure of risk? How much staff time do you use up on gathering all this information, when the more time you spend on assessment, the less you are able to spend on actually offering a service? What weightings do you give to different kinds of risk?

Beckett sees all potentially risky situations as a pyramid with a large number being relatively low risk at the base and a relatively small number being high risk at the peak. Because the pyramid depicts risk rather than certainty however, people categorised as low risk may, in fact, turn out to be dangerous while those thought of as high risk do not. Beckett argues that risk assessment essentially entails drawing a line across the pyramid with the notion that above the line people are more likely to be dangerous while below the line they are not. However, no matter how carefully those assessing the risk draw the line it is not going to be one hundred percent accurate and a different line across the pyramid represents the extent of the true risk (i.e. showing harm that actually results). The fact that the two lines representing perception and reality are different means that there will inevitably be false negatives (those thought not to be dangerous who turn out to be so) and false positives (those thought to be dangerous who turn out to be safe).

It is important to recognise that different risks exist for different people at different times and in different contexts. A mental health worker may be comforted by the thought that someone will be less at risk of being a danger to themselves if admitted compulsorily to the apparent comparative safety of a hospital ward environment. Hird and Cash (2000) however, argue that the service user may see the notion of risk quite differently. There is a risk to self-esteem arising from the loss of autonomy that a compulsory admission entails. There are risks of unwanted side effects from medical treatments and other risks from violence, victimisation and abuse on hospital wards. People do also kill themselves while detained in supposedly secure environments. This is ironic as well as tragic if they were admitted to these places in order to keep them alive in the first place. No course of action, or inaction, is risk-free.

It could therefore be argued that the notion of risk assessment could offer a false sense of reassurance in that people may be deceived into thinking they have dealt with a potential risk when they have not. There is now plentiful material available advising social workers and others in the caring professions how they can stay safe (see for example Bibby, 1994; Braithwaite, 2001). However, workers may become complacent, thinking that they can read the helpful leaflet or in-house violence and aggression policy later and never actually get around to doing so. One of the consequences of fear is that people, however well informed they may be before the event, forget what they know and find even the most carefully assimilated information unavailable to them at times of need because of the ways in which fear blocks thought. De-Becker (1997) argues that feeling-based intuition is frequently likely to be of more help to people under threat than a more cognitively-based risk assessment. The ideal combination could be seen as a form of cognitive risk assessment that makes due allowance for the crucial importance of intuition. Risk assessment can be a helpful servant but an inappropriate and unbalanced master. Its principal advantage is that it builds in a space and time to anticipate and hypothesise what may happen in the future on the basis of what is known from the past.

Recommendations for good practice in risk assessment and risk management

- Identify the hazards; who may be harmed and how? Evaluate the risks and options for support. Does more need to be done?
- Always be aware of your own safety needs and the effects of decisions and actions upon these.
- Work in partnership by allowing appropriate others to contribute to final decisions.
- Record plans clearly and score risks on dimensions of anticipated likelihood and significance.
- Recognise the limitations of risk assessment and allow for the importance of intuition.
- Recognise that service users are likely to perceive a different type of risk than professionals.
- Anticipate defending your decisions to act or refrain from acting to an inquiry at some future date. Therefore record criteria used for decision making.
- Act in good faith and without negligence.
- After the event review what worked well and what not so well. Amend policy and practice accordingly.

CHAPTER 7

Support, consultation, supervision, de-briefing

This chapter begins with a consideration of the support needs of EDT workers and an acknowledgement of potential difficulties for managers and supervisors charged with the responsibility of providing this support. As most EDTs rarely undertake planned work supervision of casework, such as it is, will usually take place while the work is unfolding or after the event. Sometimes it may be necessary to think of staff needs for de-briefing after traumatic events. EDTs will often consider ways in which they can improve working relationships with systems they work with such as partner agencies and daytime teams. Models of internal individual and group supervision are discussed and the chapter concludes with recommendations for good practice.

Supporting the lone worker

One of the main differences most frequently experienced and commented upon by social workers changing from daytime to out of hours work is the relative isolation of the EDT worker and the greater autonomy that the EDT role confers. Even though management cover may be sparse during the day it is still usually possible to contact a manager when absolutely necessary. Indeed, it is often a requirement that this is so. Despite the fact that EDTs cover at least 75 per cent of a working week, much more thought is given to the gate-keeping systems and procedures that function within weekday working hours than outside them. For example, in order to accommodate a child or admit an older person into a residential establishment, a daytime worker will often need to gain agreement from various levels of management before presenting their case to a panel. Out of normal office hours however, an EDT worker may be able to achieve these outcomes either entirely without consultation or after only a brief telephone call to a manager. Despite the ostensible acknowledgement that such crises do occur out of hours there is comparatively little thought given to their resolution, almost as if the possible difficulties are denied sufficiently then they won't materialise. Another example of 'out of sight, out of mind'.

Most EDTs have a manager or team leader but that person may not have the authority necessary to agree to a resource being committed or monies from a budget being spent. It then becomes necessary to gain access to a person with this authority. Daytime managers may no wish to be available on an organised rota to be contacted out of hours, especially if they will not be paid for this, but some might agree to being spoken to if they are actually in when the need arises. This (lack of a) system means that EDT workers can sometimes waste long periods of time leaving messages on ansaphones whilst trying to contact appropriate people. Sometimes such delays might have beneficial consequences but usually they are highly undesirable and attract the chagrin of the police who have a far more tightly defined hierarchy of decision making with contact arrangements specified for ranks at all levels of authority.

Some situations faced by EDT workers may evoke particularly strong responses. The possibility that workers might be personally affected by or identify with particular cases has been mentioned in Chapter 2. Powerful feelings may resonate with individuals at various times pertinent to their own life experiences. The loss of a child, difficulties with an adolescent, illness, separation or caring for an older relative are commonly-found examples. If there are two EDT workers on duty in an office base at the same time they can 'watch out' for one another. Sometimes workers may be so affected by a perceived attack that they find themselves shouting down the telephone at the caller. They may not realise that they are doing so until their colleague, sitting nearby, points this out. Sometimes workers 'snap' as a result of feeling that inappropriate or excessive demands are being made of them by people who are being unreasonable. Complaints may then be threatened by the caller and encouraged by the worker, temporarily in an angry, defiant and retaliatory mood. If an EDT worker is alone when receiving a difficult call with no one else available to notice how they are being affected, it is sometimes helpful for them to cultivate a reflective process described by Casement (1985) as 'internal supervision'.

Internal supervision

Casement (1985), who was a social worker before becoming a psycho-analyst, coined the term 'internal supervision' to describe a process whereby therapists 'internalised' a good and helpful supervisor whom they could 'consult' in their mind whilst situations were developing. Most supervision is retrospective and relies upon the supervisee's memory and accounts about what happened and who said what when. This model has limitations; not only is memory notoriously fallible (Ofshe and Watters, 1995), but supervisees are likely, knowingly or unknowingly, to present themselves and their actions in a relatively favourable light. They can also choose which material to introduce and discuss and which to omit, edit or modify. Because the internal supervisor is part of the supervisee, created and generated by them, there is less likelihood of conscious deception as, were they to present situations inappropriately or partially the supervisee would only be fooling themselves.

In order to consult with and listen to the internal supervisor the worker needs knowingly to dissociate to some extent. Whilst listening to what service users are saying workers need simultaneously to access that part of their thinking which is consciously evaluating what is being said, and to check this out with their internal supervisor. An example is:

> Service user: *(Raging, angry, and immediately demanding) 'I've had enough of my 15 year-old daughter. She's been taking drugs, missing school, sleeping with older men and stealing. Tonight she just threw her younger brother down the stairs and I've hit her. If you don't come round here right now and take her away I'm going to kill her and it will be your fault.'*

> Worker: *(Thinks: I need to check out if this family is known, what's the history, what's the care plan (if any), is the child on the child protection register, what is the extent and seriousness of the injuries to the young woman and her brother – do they need medical attention . . . ?) 'Could you give me your name, address and telephone number?' (These are given). 'Have you had any contact with social services before?'*

> Service user: *'Don't give me all that. I've told you all you need to know – come round now or you'll be sorry.'*

> Worker: *'I'm willing to try and help you with this situation but before I can do this I need some more basic information from you first.'*

> Service user: *'I'm sick of you lot – paid for nothing – just sitting there on your backsides all day, doing nothing, you never do* anything. . . . *You come round here now or I'm going to the newspapers . . .'*

> Worker: *(Feels himself getting increasingly angry at being given so little opportunity to respond appropriately, feels that service user is being rude and bullying, feels partly like terminating the call ('I don't have to be spoken to like this – this is verbal abuse'), but is also partly concerned for the well-being of the children concerned and anxious as to how the situation will resolve. While remaining on the telephone listening to the service user he decides to consult his internal supervisor and tells them the above).*

> Internal supervisor: *The first thing to do is to breathe deeply, stay calm, remain professional. Whatever happens the situation is not going to be helped by you getting angry. It's often a good technique in these situations, first of all, to acknowledge the emotion expressed and see where that gets you. Shelve your need for details for the time being, concentrate on empathising with what the service user is saying and take it from there.*

> Worker: *(to service user) 'All this must make you very angry . . .'*

> Service user: *'You can say that again!'*

> Worker: *'. . . and I guess you feel that your daughter has no right to treat you like this.'*

> Service user: *'Absolutely . . . If you had any idea of all I've done for her . . .'*

Internal supervisor: *(to social worker)* 'That's good, now you are building rapport. Stay with the feelings, get him to talk more about their relationship.'

Worker: *(to service user)* 'Tell me more about that . . .'

Whatever happens from this point onwards the social worker has now established rapport with the service user and they are communicating co-operatively. Once people's strong emotions have been acknowledged and validated they are capable of changing entirely their perception of the situation and their responses to it (see the example in Chapter 1 of the mother who began by saying she would happily see her 15-year-old dead and, an hour later was co-operating in having him returned from the police back into her care). Covey (1992) argues that the principle of seeking first to understand before needing to be understood is the single most important factor contributing to successful negotiations between human beings. The internal supervisor can help in this process and by cultivating its working has advantages similar to those of reflection-in-action advocated by Schon (1983) whose writing underpins the reflective thinking and practice encouraged in contemporary social work (Yelloly and Henkel, 1995).

Practice of using the internal supervisor is especially important for EDT workers since an actual supervisor is unlikely to be available for immediate consultation. Even if supervisors and managers were more easily contactable it is possible that they would not be used because EDT workers often pride themselves on their autonomy, independence and self-sufficiency. This can cause difficulties for managers and supervisors who are expected to ensure quality standards.

The role of managers and supervisors

The autonomy and independence required for much EDT work has led to claims that some EDTs operate in a 'macho' culture and are staffed by 'maverick' workers. EDTs function outside the mainstream daytime system and for those who work from home there is not even an office setting to remind them that they are part of a wider bureaucracy which works within established policies and procedures. The managers of some EDTs may work as practitioner-managers and fill shifts on the rota on a regular or occasional basis. They are therefore closer to and more immediately engaged in issues of actual practice. This practitioner role helps them to be aware first-hand of the difficulties, dilemmas and constraints faced by team members. For those who work in teams, the manager/supervisor and team member/supervisee will be working across a desk from one another. This affords the manager or supervisor an opportunity to directly observe their team members at work. Because of this they will be able to see and experience for themselves the functioning reality of their workers' practice. This gives them an advantage over other supervisors who work with a traditional model of supervision whereby they rely upon what they are told by the supervisee. This way of working also means that the manager/supervisor's practice is observed and experienced directly by team members who will form opinions about this. The practitioner-manager style of working in teams should therefore aid greater transparency of both worker and manager but personality clashes might make for more problematic and guarded behaviours and practice.

In contrast to this the EDT manager/supervisor is often themselves managed by someone more remote. Senior management arrangements for EDTs can frequently change if the team is slotted into different categories of organisational structures at different times for different reasons. The management of EDT arguably fits anywhere and belongs nowhere. Because the majority of work undertaken is mental health or child care work there are arguments to suggest that the team should be managed within adult or children's portfolios and teams are often moved around between the two. This gives senior managers little time to come to develop understanding of the complexities and vagaries of EDT work and the personalities and style of the team before there is another reorganisation and the team's management is changed again. Also, given the busy lives of most senior managers, if complaints are few and the work seems to be carried out to most people's satisfaction most of the time, EDTs are likely to be left alone and attract little attention. This process reinforces and encourages the independent, 'macho' style and culture mentioned earlier.

It is not uncommon for EDT workers to have at least 20 years post-qualifying experience each. This can make it hard to supervise such workers as they are undoubtedly knowledgeable, skilled and experienced. There may be a temptation to think that they can be left alone to get on with work responsibly and that they will make it known if they want or need help. Nevertheless, in its study of *Inquiry Reports into Child Abuse 1980–1989* the Department of Health (1991) warns against complacency when considering the needs of even very experienced workers for supervision. Any worker is liable to get things wrong, forget something important or have their judgement clouded for a variety of reasons and EDT workers are not immune from this. The encouragement of life-long learning, and the requirement for monitored and continuing personal development is not popular with all. Some people resent the implication that they are not managing their work properly when they have not received a serious complaint by anyone for many years. Others see the chance to update their skills and knowledge in a more positive light. The recent emphasis on life-long learning has implication for the training of EDT workers and this subject is considered in Chapter 5.

Part of the supervisor's role is to ensure that recording is of a satisfactory standard. The practitioner-manager will come across case notes in a random fashion when working shifts and will thereby form an opinion as to their quality and appropriateness. Additionally, a routine checking of examples of case recording can be required and planned in to regular supervision sessions. Because EDT case notes are sent to someone within the organisation either for information or action the next working day there is an in-built de facto quality control mechanism. Someone will have to read them and colleagues are usually quick to make it known if they find some aspect of recording unclear or unsatisfactory. Colleagues are also in a position to influence how EDT record their involvement to some extent so that their recording systems and preferences are followed and enhanced so far as is possible.

Apart from managing quality control good supervision will also comprise challenge, support and looking at career development. It will focus on the needs of the service user, practitioner and organisation (Hughes and Pengelly, 1998). EDT work is replete with challenges and most workers will experience some kind of challenge on most shifts. Supervisors do not therefore have to seek out challenges to keep their workers stimulated. All workers will have some established prejudices and favoured ways of responding to situations, and these would benefit from a fresh look or re-appraisal from time-to-time. The disadvantage of being seen as competent, capable and efficient is that workers may become complacent and set in their ways for want of a 'newcomer's perspective' on the work they undertake. Linking supervision with an annual appraisal helps to clear a dedicated time once a year when the appraisee's work can be thought about and career development needs can be considered. EDTs commonly have students on placement (see chapter 5) and these attachments can help to introduce a constant questioning of what would otherwise be taken for granted. As has been shown throughout this book, EDT workers are liable to encounter sudden and disturbing traumas and tragedies throughout the course of their work. One question for employers charged with the responsibility of providing a duty of care to their workers is how to support their employees through these times.

De-briefing after exposure to traumatic events

EDT workers need to be independent, autonomous and resilient. Because they are on duty so frequently on their own they need to be professionally capable and personally strong. Nevertheless, some of the situations they need to deal with would test the capabilities of any worker. Murder, suicide, sadism, cruelty, torture and perversion are all likely to come to the attention of EDT workers, often in graphic and explicit detail. It is essential that these situations are responded to immediately and their ensuing aftermath dealt with properly. For those working in a team, colleagues on duty together can help support and advise one another. This has the advantage that those working the shift together will have been aware of situations as they developed and will have probably discussed the ongoing management of a case as new information emerged. The need for immediate consultation and decision making is paramount in these circumstances. On rare occasions a manager may be contacted either because they need to know of a serious situation, such as the death of a child in care, or because some form of guidance or advice is necessary. Usually, however, EDT workers will decide for themselves how to proceed and this is expected of them.

One of the difficulties of dealing with trauma is that it is often hard to gauge the true extent to which an incident has affected a worker. Health and social care workers remember traumatic incidents for many years after they have happened (Smith and Nursten, 1995; Buyssen, 1996) and it is often only with the passing of time that one begins to appreciate the extent of impact that incidents have had. Freud (1930: 69) writes, 'In mental life nothing which has once been formed can perish – everything is somehow preserved and in suitable circumstances it can once more be brought to light.' People remember events with a cinematic eye for detail and can easily talk at great length about things that happened to them decades ago, as if it were yesterday (Smith and Nursten, 1998). This says something about the way in which memories of traumatic experiences are stored in the mind and the effect that they have on thinking and functioning whether the individual is consciously aware of them at the time or not.

When acting as an appropriate adult under The Police and Criminal Evidence Act 1984 one female EDT worker had to listen to graphic and intricate details of how a male service user tortured and eventually killed his female partner. Another worker having responded in the aftermath of two murders in previous weeks was called to assess a service user under The Mental Health Act 1983. The man in question had tried to kill himself by pushing a knife down through his eye socket and out of his mouth. The assessment took place with the knife still in position and his face covered in blood. Sometimes the trauma may not be so obvious but triggers off a personal experience so that the work requiring attention assumes a 'threatening' nature (Smith and Nursten, 1998). It is also likely that however well an EDT worker gets on with their colleagues or manager they will not have shared such a private experience with them so others cannot be aware of the personal meanings and associations which may be elicited or resurrected by such situations.

When finishing shifts late at night few workers will return home from an EDT office and go straight to bed. There is usually a need to settle down and process the events of the shift before being able to rest. If the shift has been particularly difficult there may be a wish to talk about what has happened with someone and it is not often easy to find trusted confidants available when shifts end. However, it is important, regardless of the experience and capability of the worker, to make due allowance for the need to think through and process traumatic material. Workers may seem to be OK, it may look as if things have been dealt with, but then they have an accident or illness of some kind which may be their way of expressing their need for help.

Sometimes, if an incident affects a sufficient number of professionals, a health trust or social services department may provide a formal de-briefing whereby those involved can share what they did or did not do and their associated perceptions, thoughts and feelings. More often, an individual is left to identify support needs for themselves and to seek these out. A frequently raised question for supervisors and supervisees is the extent to which they want to explore such responses to trauma even if their relationship was sufficiently conducive to doing so. People can be very vulnerable and raw in the aftermath of traumatic events, particularly as these may well have triggered previous experiences of trauma. They may say things to a supervisor which they later come to regret, and, when they feel stronger, may come to resent the supervisor for seeing them so low and exposed (Smith and Nursten, 1998; Smith, 2000). It is therefore helpful for supervisors to know when to refer on, perhaps to occupational health services or for specialist counselling outside the organisation so that the individual can be responded to in confidence and anonymity. If doing this however, it is also important to recognise the need to maintain an ongoing professional interest and concern so that the worker does not feel that they have been 'passed on' or discarded. Offers of support may not be taken up at the time but months later, workers might make it known that they appreciated the offer being made. This suggests that the knowledge that the support is there if needed may suffice to the extent that it is not actually necessary to make use of it.

A regular, planned supervisory meeting with EDT workers provides a dedicated opportunity to discuss traumatic events in retrospect. While the immediate needs presented by the case will have been addressed, exploration and full appreciation of the aftermath of trauma may yet be considered to benefit within the appropriate confines of the supervisory relationship. Because so little EDT work is planned, supervision is not used to anticipate likely happenings and demands within individual cases as it is in much daytime work. Casework supervision in EDTs is therefore mostly retrospective and reactive. Even so, EDTs do work frequently with daytime teams and other partner agencies and this work can be planned in an organised and systematic manner.

Forward planning for work with teams and systems

A major challenge for EDTs is the need to keep up to date with the quantity and different types of information necessary to function effectively out of normal office hours. There are rotas for many different people in various organisations whose boundaries are rarely co-terminus with the area covered by an EDT (see Chapter 8). Because of the range of people who potentially need to be contacted, the pace of change in most services, and the geographical variations and different preferences that exist in different localities, it takes time and organisation to keep up to date with and maintain access to necessary information. EDTs are in equal danger of being told too little or too much. They will sometimes be omitted from circulation lists notifying important policy changes (out of sight, out of mind again), despite repeated attempts to ensure that this does not happen. Alternatively they may be sent policies and procedures circulated to daytime teams written with a depth of specialist knowledge and detail that they do not have or will not need. Too much information is as unhelpful as too little; when needing to make decisions out of hours in a crisis, there is not the time available to sift through great detail whilst trying to extract the essentially relevant points. Most documents written by daytime teams, for example child protection conference notes, are not written with a view to yielding crucial information necessary for a crisis response and EDTs constantly need to balance the value of understanding the detail of the bigger picture with the constraints of time and need to make decisions quickly.

To aid relationships with daytime teams and services operating out of normal office hours, EDTs might operate a system of liaison arrangements. This work may be undertaken by the EDT manager, attending crucial policy and strategy meetings relevant to out of hours work. Alternatively roles may be shared out between team members who each take responsibility for liaising at 'grass roots' level with different teams, services or policy areas. This enables the manager to get involved only when necessary and to attend more strategic level meetings. Liaison work undertaken by team members has the advantage that all EDT members gain awareness of, and work to bridge gaps that may exist between those services operating at night and those in the day. Members of different teams get to meet one another face-to-face and thereby establish relationships which might prove useful later when negotiating difficult situations. Although individuals within teams change over time, the principle of being able to talk about crisis responses, away from the heat of the crisis, is a useful one.

If an EDT does have a system of liaison roles these are likely to be discussed in the supervision of EDT workers:

- What difficulties exist with X service user group?
- What new information/system/policy/procedure has come into being that we need to respond to?
- Have there been requests for EDT to work in a different way?
- Who needs to do what in order to improve the functioning of working relationships?

These and other questions are likely to be considered as part of the monitoring and supervision of liaison roles. Because of this, management of EDT workers may also include supervision of planned work with agencies, teams and systems. This resembles the way in which supervisors of daytime teams attempt to think about and anticipate developments in casework with individuals. Liaison work is also a constant feature of discussion when EDTs meet together as a team.

Group and individual supervision

EDT meetings (sometimes held in daytime hours) afford a rare opportunity for all team members to get together. Agenda items will often include planning for shifts to be worked on future rotas and negotiating changes to existing rotas. Because people frequently want to change when they had previously agreed to work for a variety of reasons, swapping shifts and negotiating changes is a major part of most meetings. Liaison issues and roles will be discussed. Team meetings provide useful opportunities to invite visitors from other teams and services so that different perspectives and constraints can be appreciated and any difficulties in working together can be discussed. As well as dealing with the day-to-day/night-to-night routine business (the kitchen sink and provision of milk often feature on a regular basis) team meetings also offer an opportunity for group supervision.

It is said that groups can be greater than the sum of their parts. This is particularly likely to be true of EDT groups as, all team members including the manager, are on duty alone covering the entire designated area. At some time they *are* the social services. In this respect there is an implicit equality of status and people regard themselves and each other as each having a valid contribution to make to discussions. A group supervision session may be spontaneous or planned and arises when a particular issue, theme/aspect of work, or case appears to merit shared attention. Examples of such sessions include:

- How to respond sensitively to the needs of students on placement in the team.
- Who should do what, and to what extent, if the nominated practice teacher is not on a shift but their student is?
- How should team members respond to a particular policy that is causing repeated difficulties?
- Given the variety in styles of work conducted by various members of EDT how can team members respond consistently to repeat callers so that one individual's response does not set up a precedent which causes difficulties for others?
- How can we better understand the needs of one particular service user group, for example, young people who self-harm?
- Are there common, good practice principles which we can all aim to work to?

The advantage of group supervision is that for a particular topic under consideration a variety of perspectives is obtained from different people who are known to have experience and credibility in the subject. Sometimes EDT members will prefer to put an item on the agenda for group supervision rather than raise it in individual supervision. Although people are strong individuals within the team, they also simultaneously work as part of a team; when they respond as themselves they are also responding on behalf of the team. Group supervision within a team meeting is a useful forum in which team members can work out this individual/team dynamic.

This chapter now concludes with a summary of good practice principles regarding support and supervision within an EDT context.

Recommendations for good practice in support and supervision

- The needs of EDT workers for support, supervision and consultation should not be over-looked regardless of their individual experience and capability.
- EDT workers should develop a capacity for 'reflection-in-action' and an understanding of how to consult with their 'internal supervisor'.
- There should be understanding of ways in which case work issues may resonate with worker's auto-biographical experiences – both personal and professional.
- Allowance should be made for the equal and opposite dangers of workers feeling omnipotent and impotent.
- The effects of isolation of the lone worker should be recognised and addressed in ways that do not undermine individuality and autonomy.

- The EDT manager and other appropriate managers should be available for support and consultation when the need arises.
- EDT managers/supervisors may be helped in their work if they also work as practitioners alongside their supervisees.
- Recording should be regularly checked and high standards maintained.
- Supervision should comprise support, challenge, and consideration of career development.
- Supervisors should recognise the possible need for referring on to external counsellors/de-briefers for workers affected by traumatic events when necessary.
- Peer support should be appreciated and harnessed effectively.
- Liaison roles should be clearly identified and appropriately supervised.
- The value of group as well as individual supervision should be recognised.

Working Together

CHAPTER 8

Partnership working

This chapter is concerned with the need for partnership working between agencies and organisations. It begins with a survey of the wide range of different agencies and individuals with whom EDTs need to work in partnership and demonstrates why effective partnership working agreements are necessary. It is acknowledged that conflict will arise between partners from time to time and the need to make appropriate allowances for this, and to move on is explained. The 'container function' of partnership working at its best is then demonstrated followed by consideration of how the wheels of partnerships can best be oiled and maintained. The chapter ends with some recommendations intended to promote best practice in partnership working.

The need for effective partnerships

The number of different people and agencies that EDTs need to work with is considerable and might include:

- The emergency services – police, ambulance and fire.
- General practitioners, health visitors and district nurses.
- Psychiatrists and other doctors approved under section 12 of the Mental Health Act.
- NHS Direct call centres.
- Hospitals, particularly accident and emergency departments.
- Schools, education welfare officers.
- Foster carers.
- Probation officers.
- Solicitors and magistrate's courts.
- The Benefits Agency (Department of Work and Pensions).
- Housing officers and housing provision, hostels and women's aid refuges.
- Home care and private providers of domiciliary care.
- Care support workers working in the community out of hours.
- Residential Units.
- The Home Office with regard to asylum seekers and social supervision of mental health patients.

- Interpreters.
- Chaplains and other religious leaders/institutions.
- Emergency planning officers.
- Taxi firms and escorting services.
- Daytime social services colleagues and their managers.
- Voluntary agencies such as the NSPCC, Childline, Shelterline, Saneline.
- Other EDTs.

Not only do EDTs need to know what each of these people/agencies do and how they operate, they need also to recognise the considerable variations in practice that might exist between the 'same' service operating in different geographical areas. One EDT covered an area which included three different youth offending teams. Although each was, ostensibly, engaged in the 'same' work they functioned quite differently from one another with practices reflecting the needs and demands of their local populations, their staffing levels and their own interpretation of legislation and codes of practice.

The need for effective partnership work in child protection is explained by the Department of Health (1999b: 2) 'Promoting children's well-being and safeguarding them from significant harm depends crucially upon effective information sharing, collaboration and understanding between agencies and professionals. Constructive relationships between individual workers need to be supported by a strong lead from elected or appointed authority members, and the commitment of chief officers'. The same need for efficient and integrated care is equally relevant to work between EDTs and all service user groups.

It is apparent from previous chapters how closely EDTs need to work with other agencies, especially the police and health colleagues. The principle of effective partnership is apparent in the multi-agency approach to child protection training and practice. It can also be seen in the composition of youth offending and community mental health teams where different disciplines are brought together in the same building under one manager. The creation of primary care trusts in England and health and social services boards in Northern Ireland further reflects the underlying acceptance of the partnership principle.

Because EDT workers often work alone or with just one other colleague out of hours they may have difficulty in feeling that they are part of a wider social work community. They identify their work as being more within the network of that provided by other services and might come to regard health and police colleagues as closer operational co-workers than other social workers. When partnerships work well they are satisfying and rewarding, delivering effective integrated thinking and action. Each partner performs their particular and unique function so that the whole operation proves greater than the sum of its parts and service users receive holistic consideration and appropriate responses. Examples of effective partnership working can be found in Chapters

2, 3 and 4, whilst Chapter 5 shows how training together with partners can not only consolidate relationships but also beneficially influence working practices.

Sometimes though, partners might wish to work together but pressure of work and other demands make this difficult as is illustrated in the following instance:

A man in his fifties with a history of manic-depressive illness, whose wife suffered from an advanced form of a degenerative disease, suddenly made known his intention to travel with his wife to a distant hotel at 8 p.m. one Sunday evening. It appeared that he had entered a manic phase of his illness since he showed no acknowledgement of the severity of his wife's condition or the fact that she could not safely travel far at night. The man was known to have assaulted his general practitioner when unwell previously. Therefore, when arranging for a mental health act assessment to take place at 6 p.m. the EDT worker concerned requested that the police should also attend.

The EDT worker met with two doctors outside the man's house at 6 p.m. The police were not there and explained that, because of their need to attend to other priorities, they would be unable attend for at least another hour. Since the man had made clear his intention to leave at 8 p.m. the situation had become urgent. The EDT worker and doctors needed to determine whether the risk would be too great if they should begin the assessment process without the police, knowing that they could call 999 if the situation became unsafe. This called for a fine judgement. The knowledge that people who have been violent in the past are most likely to repeat this behaviour on future occasions (Braithwaite, 2001; Mason and Chandley, 2001) needed to be balanced with the recognition that just because someone has been violent previously it does not necessarily predict that they will be so again. The EDT worker and doctors assessed the risks (see Chapter 6) reasoning that they did not know how the man would respond to them on that particular evening. They decided to test this by knocking on the door, gauging his response, proceeding accordingly, and withdrawing if necessary.

In fact the man let the EDT worker and doctors in and, after relaxing and co-operating increasingly as the interview proceeded, he talked about how he saw his situation and what his plans were. It was apparent after a short time that he needed admission to hospital. His wife, although used to his mood swings, was frightened of him and concerned for her own safety should he carry out his stated plan to take her away with him. The prevailing difficulty was that he lacked the capacity to consent to a voluntary admission and was likely to become violent when informed that admission was thought necessary. Although the EDT worker and doctors had judged it appropriate to conduct the initial assessment, they did not feel sufficiently safe to tell the service user the outcome of their assessment without police back-up. They also thought that to do so may be irresponsible should the man be provoked into violent or disturbed behaviour.

By now it was 7 p.m. and the EDT worker and doctors left the house asking the man and his wife not to go away before they returned to discuss the situation further. Again, they requested police assistance. Two policemen arrived at 7.15 p.m. After learning the circumstances of the case they expressed their willingness to support the EDT worker and doctors but did not think it advisable to do so without the attendance of an ambulance crew. They pointed out that ambulances can sometimes take in excess of two hours to respond to a request to transport a patient detained under the Mental Health Act and, if this man should need restraining, as seemed likely, it would be wholly inappropriate to do this for two hours or more. The ambulance control was contacted but was unable to respond immediately because of other priorities. They said an ambulance could attend at 9 p.m. and so the EDT worker and police officers agreed to meet outside the house again then. By this time a helpful and understanding neighbour had become involved. Having been party to a number of the service user's previous difficult admissions, and being concerned for the wife, this neighbour had a good idea of the process involved and agreed to sit with the couple and attempt to ensure that the man did not leave the house with his wife.

At 9 p.m. the EDT worker returned to the house to find the ambulance ready and waiting but no police officers had arrived. He was told that they were unable to attend because of other competing priorities. The ambulance crew waited until 9.20 p.m. and then said that they needed to go to attend to other work. Fortunately, the police arrived just at that time and the admission was successfully effected shortly afterwards.

This case is a good example of the number of partner agencies and individuals that may need to co-operate when responding to crises arising out of hours. The EDT worker needed to work with the doctors and the man's wife when assessing him under the Mental Health Act. Having completed the assessment, arrangements need to be made for the police to perform their role which, in this instance, could be done safely only in conjunction with the ambulance service. A neighbour becomes helpfully and appropriately involved as part of the caring response. There is then the need for the EDT worker to follow the ambulance to the admitting hospital and to brief the receiving ward staff of the circumstances of the assessment, highlighting any difficulties they may encounter. It is also apparent from this example how the principle of partnership assumes a willingness to work together to the benefit of the service user in a spirit of mutual co-operation. There is no 'senior partner'. The approved social worker had a co-ordinating responsibility but could not insist that the police and/or the ambulance were present at a particular time. The police and ambulance services established their own priorities, through their separate hierarchies, and neither had authority to command the other's resources. Such factors can cause difficulties whilst working together and conflict may then occur between partners.

Conflict between partners

When one partner regards a situation as being of higher priority than another difficulties might arise. Shift changes can interrupt plans agreed upon by parties previously involved because individuals arriving new to a situation see it differently from their predecessors. EDT workers know that ambulance crews need to give priority to people in cardiac arrest and that available police officers may be called away to deal with a serious road traffic accident or disturbance at the local football ground but this knowledge does not help them to deal with the crisis for which they feel responsible and cannot deal with safely alone. An EDT worker might request police attendance when carrying out a child protection visit to a known difficult family or when assessing someone with a history of violence under the Mental Health Act but be told that there is no one currently available, thus making it impossible for the worker to carry out their duties safely. When partnerships work well they are advantageous for all concerned. Like all close relationships however, partnerships are not, and cannot be, trouble free. There are inevitably times of conflict between partners.

The complexity of working in partnership with the number of agencies (potentially) involved in any given locality is highlighted by the Department of Health (2001: 70):

> *There are 33 councils responsible for social services within London. These councils work in partnership with 4,400 GPs, 15 Primary Care Trusts, 35 Primary Care Groups, 59 NHS Trusts and 14 Health Authorities to improve the health and well-being of the London population . . . Although there are obvious benefits from the localised arrangements for delivering health and social care, given the complex and diverse nature of the population including high mobility, there are difficulties in managing and co-ordinating services across boundaries.*

When the full list of diverse agencies with whom EDTs work (see above) is considered alongside the complexities of working with various health providers, the scale of partnership working (and the different ways in which this can cause conflict) is apparent.

Whenever several agencies are involved with the same service users, there is always the possibility of one being 'played off' against the other and any inconsistencies in their various responses being exploited. Service users might ask EDTs for something that their daytime worker has previously refused. If the EDT has been informed of this and accept the reasons for that refusal they can respond accordingly. If they are not fully informed they may perceive the request to be a reasonable one and grant it to the subsequent chagrin of the daytime worker. Whenever there is partnership there is also the possibility of division. Professionals meetings are sometimes convened to agree upon a consistent response to problematic callers but it is often difficult for all main parties to attend such meetings. Therefore information might not be communicated or made available to the person who needs to know it at a crucial time.

The police will provide an immediate response to crisis situations and are empowered by legislation to ensure immediate protection when this is thought to be necessary (see Chapters 2 and 3). Having made an initial response the police usually then rely on appropriate partner agencies to take over from them and to address the ongoing needs of the individual. For instance, a police officer might use powers of 'police protection' to remove a child believed to be at risk in a situation perceived as dangerous or detrimental to the child's well-being. The officer will then contact EDT and can feel understandably aggrieved when told that, although the worker agrees that the child is at risk, there are no suitable places currently available in either foster care or residential care. Sometimes the outcome of such a lack of resources is that a child stays at the police station overnight. This is not in the interests of the child and frustrates the police considerably as they feel they are being used as 'childminders'. If an officer needs to stay with the child the police resent having to use their limited resources for work which is not their core business and which affects their ability to meet their own performance targets and measures.

If a police officer detains someone found in a public place under section 136 of the Mental Health Act 1983 they then need to take them to a place of safety. Such a place of safety will usually be a police station or an appropriate facility in a psychiatric hospital. While each case is judged upon its merits, it is generally the case that those thought to be a danger to themselves are more likely to be taken to hospital and those thought to pose a risk to others, perhaps by way of violent behaviour, to be taken to the police station. As with the case of police protection, cited above, the police are dependent upon others taking over from them so that they are then free to attend other situations requiring their immediate attention. It is most annoying therefore for the police to take a service user to a psychiatric hospital under section 136 to be told that the person will not be accepted because the unit has a no-alcohol policy and the person concerned has been drinking alcohol. The police might argue, that although the person has consumed some alcohol, they are not drunk. The hospital will counter that it is impossible (and illegal) to assess the mental state of anyone who has taken any amount of alcohol because the extent to which this might affect their mental state is unknowable. Again, there is no 'senior partner'. The police cannot pull rank on the hospital or vice versa. Partnership needs goodwill and compromise to work effectively and if partners are not prepared to give and take, then effective joint working cannot take place.

Guidelines and policies, outlining the limits of responsibility and detailing courses of action in particular instances can sometimes be helpful. However, even the most carefully worded policies cannot cover every eventuality and all policies are subject to interpretation. If there is sufficient ill-will and distemper partners can sabotage policies. Unfortunately staff in different roles within the caring professions can feel so demoralised and under siege that rather than turn to one another for mutual support and encouragement they turn against one another. Oppression is internalised and agencies fight with colleagues whose co-operation they need the most. Partnerships cannot flourish in such climates. Like all relationships, the greatest threat is posed by those one lives most intimately with.

There is currently an increasing emphasis on health and social care personnel working closely together and staff sharing the same manager is seen as a useful step in bringing this about. In other respects, however, the true spirit of partnership may be lacking. Computer systems (and even, sometimes, individuals) do not 'talk to each other', recording is kept separate and boundaries and responsibilities are not coterminous. Beliefs and policies about confidentiality might prevent some individuals from sharing certain information, leaving others to feel indignant and hurt that they had not been informed of something crucial. A general practitioner might insist that a patient needs admission to care but claim that this is for 'social' rather than medical reasons and therefore social services should arrange and pay it for it. An EDT worker might assess the situation differently and ensuing arguments are likely to be all the more fraught because of everyone's need to keep within budgets and to demonstrate performance outcomes. It is often easier to demonise and fight with one's partners than to attempt to understand and empathise with them.

New services, such as 'rapid response crisis intervention teams' working out of hours are being planned in some areas and might appear to be a helpful addition to existing services. If, due account is not taken of existing service provision however, such new initiatives may flounder since established teams may refuse to refer to, or work alongside, such new teams. Staffing levels in many areas of health and social care are often low (Department of Health, 2001) and new teams might be able to attract their staff only by drawing from the pool of suitably qualified people already working in existing teams, leaving them depleted and even less able to function well.

Partnership working makes good sense but in reality it can be a precarious and vulnerable arrangement. Relationships that have taken months or years to build slowly and carefully can be damaged or even destroyed in a few moments as a consequence of the wrong action by the wrong person at the wrong time. Despite the difficulties entailed with working successfully in partnership out of hours, striving for it is worthwhile as, ultimately, it is only by co-operating together that agencies can achieve their purpose. When working well, effective partnerships offer a *container function* for anxiety and disturbance far greater than that which could be achieved by any one partner alone.

The 'container function' of effective partnerships

Containment is a term originating from psychodynamic theory. Bion (1962) suggested that a baby might feel frightened for its life and cry and scream because of this fear. If picked up, held and soothed by a sensitive, attuned carer who recognises the baby's distress and yet, simultaneously, conveys that the baby is cared for, loved and will survive intact, the baby might calm down and regain its composure. But, if no carer came when the baby first screamed, or, if the carer who did come was themselves frightened, depressed, uncaring or even violent, the baby may feel confirmed in its distress and cry all the more. The first carer registers the baby's distress yet helps the baby to express it and then contain it, whereas the second carer pushes the distress back onto the baby leaving it to feel that its painful feelings cannot be understood or received (contained) by another. The inner disturbance then feels even more disturbing than was first experienced. Obholzer and Roberts (1994) claim that organisations too have a similar potential capacity for containment (or lack of it).

A question EDT workers frequently pose to themselves and others is, 'Is it sufficient that I hear, think about, record and pass on this referral, or should I take some action because of it?' Another way of expressing this is to ask whether the situation can be contained or not. The first carer in the previous example does not actually *do* anything to or for the baby other than to respond to it, hold it, receive its communication and respond (mostly) non-verbally. If the carer thought the baby might be ill then she would do something, perhaps contact a doctor. It is important to recognise that containment itself can make a significant difference to a communication even if nothing or little is actually done. EDT workers prove this to themselves time and time again (see Chapters 2 and 4 for examples) and know that simply being available to people and listening to them can bring about significant changes. However, they also need to know when a situation cannot be contained safely and where action is necessary. An example of organisations working in partnership and thereby offering containment to service users is demonstrated by the following case:

A very disturbed young woman who called EDT, on many different occasions, sometimes several times a night and throughout the early hours of the morning, saying that she was going to kill herself or had taken an overdose and/or cut her wrists. She was diagnosed as having a borderline personality disorder and was well known to the daytime services. She had actually carried out some of her previous threats, albeit erratically, and so could not be regarded as someone who made only 'empty' threats. It was notoriously difficult to predict which of her threats would actually be implemented. Close co-operation had become well-established between EDT and daytime services who communicated frequently to evaluate the current situation and agree optimal and consistent responses. Because it was impossible to ascertain whether or not the woman had taken an overdose, and, if so, how serious this might be, it was written into the care plan that, if sufficiently concerned, the EDT worker would ask an ambulance crew to call and make an assessment. The woman knew this to be the case. Ambulance crews would also ask for police assistance when visiting as she had attacked health and social care staff previously.

One night the woman telephoned EDT and said she had taken an overdose. Having elicited details of the type and quantity of medication that the woman claimed to have taken, the EDT worker judged the situation to be sufficiently serious to warrant calling an ambulance. The woman called EDT back after a short time and said that the ambulance crew had called with the police and she had told them to leave which they had done. She repeated her claim that she had taken an overdose and implied that she might go on to take yet more tablets.

It was a busy shift and the two EDT workers on duty were dealing with a number of difficult calls. When the worker heard the woman had sent the ambulance away he was exasperated. He felt his best efforts to help had been thwarted yet the woman continued to be demanding, blocking the telephone line and thus preventing others from contacting the team. He briefly and firmly told the woman that he had responded to her as agreed with the daytime team and in conjunction with partner agencies. If she was determined to reject the available assistance then there was nothing more that he could do for her. He recorded in his notes, 'As X has rejected the help available and does not meet the criteria for compulsory detention or action under common law there is nothing more that can be done.'

Once the demand from other callers had died down the worker had opportunity to reflect on these exchanges and discuss them with his colleague, working opposite. She had been partly aware of the developing situation while dealing with other work. They hypothesised the 'worst case' scenario imagining that the caller had overdosed, or did go on to overdose, and subsequently died. This technique of projecting oneself into the future, envisaging the worst possible outcome, and 'looking back' on decisions made to see how well they bear critical scrutiny can be a useful device as part of undertaking a risk assessment (see Chapter 6). The recording in the notes that, '. . . there is nothing more that can be done . . .' seemed final. Too final; ominous even. As the workers talked the matter through they also realised that the comment was not actually true. More could be done. They considered their options:

1. They could call the service user back.
2. They could share their concerns with a manager.
3. They could contact the emergency services' personnel who attended the service user, discuss their concerns and share the risk with them.

They decided against calling the woman back for two reasons: It would give a 're-enforcing' message to her inappropriate use of the team or she might deliberately not answer the telephone thereby escalating concern. The ultimate principle to follow in these cases when workers doubt their professional judgement is to act in good faith and without negligence (Mental Health Act, 1983: section 139). Part of not being negligent is to share concerns within a professional network whilst appropriately respecting confidentiality. The workers therefore contacted the ambulance and police officers who had visited the woman. They reported that they had found her conscious, apparently well, sociable and appropriate in her communication. They doubted that she had actually taken an overdose. Having made this contact the workers then called the EDT manager. She confirmed they had done all they could in the circumstances and could not suggest any further feasible action.

These later contacts were then recorded in the notes following the statement that, '. . . nothing more can be done . . .' demonstrating that more could be, and had been, done. The service user, however, was not included in this nor was she made aware of it. The additional work that had been done was to get beyond the workers' initial frustration and eventually to be able to think further about the needs of the service user. Concerns and professional judgements had been shared between the EDT workers, with their manager, and within wider partnership relationships. Several views are frequently better than one and by thoroughly exploring all the available possibilities they had been able to share concerns and responsibilities with one another. They had also offered others the possibility of seeing something they had missed or suggesting something they had not thought of. This is one of the greatest advantages of partnership working when professionals co-operate and share their different perspectives, expertise and experiences. There is a 'containing' within the network of relationships which is greater than that which any individual could achieve alone.

Just as an observer will make a difference to any situation they observe, even if they say and do nothing, thinking things through and sharing these thoughts with partners can make a difference in the lives of service users even if they remain unaware of the thinking undertaken on their behalf. On this occasion a lull in other work made space for reflection on the situation and discussion of this by the two workers on duty. When there are not such lulls or workers are alone, identifying the need and finding the space for such reflection is more problematic, yet, nonetheless essential. In this case not only did the service user live through the night but she repeated her claim to have overdosed to the EDT workers on duty the following evening!

The advantages of good partnership working are so considerable that it is in the interests of all partners to think together as to how these can be maximised to the benefit of all concerned.

Oiling the wheels of partnership working

When partners fall out with one another there can be a tendency to send off critical letters or accusatory e-mails. While such communications may provide short-term feelings of relief, release and justification they are not usually helpful in the longer term. Once written and delivered communications cannot be altered or revoked and might be used to create further difficulties later. People, especially when angry, will sometimes send strongly expressed e-mails carrying critical and negative messages of a kind they would never express if talking to someone in person. (The speed with which e-mails can be devised, written and sent is a potential disadvantage in this respect.) For this reason making complaints either by telephone or by meeting a person to talk face-to-face is often a preferable first step to take when addressing difficulties in partnership working. Hastily sent written communications may later come back to haunt the sender and ultimately result in more harm than good.

Misunderstandings are frequently born of ignorance. One police inspector protested angrily about the lack of an EDT response one night when he wanted something done quickly and no one suitable was available. Following subsequent discussions about this instance he came to meet with the EDT manager at the EDT base. On seeing the small, one-roomed office from which the one or two EDT workers covered the whole county for all social services referrals he said, 'I'm amazed. I thought you had an all-singing, all-dancing operation here, like police control where there are lots of people working together to do different things with the capacity of calling in others for additional help in busy times'. Simply seeing the reality of the office base made a significant difference to his perceptions in this case showing how people's imaginations will often supply images in the absence of reality and how they will be influenced by what they imagine. An EDT worker answering the telephone by giving their name followed by 'Emergency Duty *Team*' may unwittingly convey a misleading impression about working as part of a fully fledged team when there is often only one person on duty at a time.

When joint working goes well letters of thanks and appreciation to partners are often relevant and can be morale-boosting. People in the caring professions do not frequently receive accolades or even appreciation and all workers benefit from meaningfully conveyed gratitude at appropriate times. Portfolios such as those compiled for the post-qualifying award in child care can be enhanced by the inclusion of service user feedback (see Chapter 9) and testimonials from partner agencies as these help provide the 'evidence base' necessary for fair assessment. Such feedback can be an aid to effective partnership working because professionals need to ask their partners and co-workers to detail and review their experiences of working together and the dialogue can be instructive and beneficial.

Effective partnership working is not achieved by one partner unthinkingly and unquestioningly going along with the views and methods of another. When partners come together to consider possible options, for example, whether a child should be placed or remain under police protection, (see Chapter 2) or whether someone should be detained under the Mental Health Act (see Chapter 3), constructive debate between partners is healthy. This is acknowledged in one of the recommendations made by Lord Laming in the Victoria Climbie inquiry (2003: 98) 'The training of social workers must equip them with the confidence to question the opinion of professionals in other agencies when conducting their own assessment of the needs of the child.' This quotation illustrates the fact that effective partnership working may be achieved as much by expression of robust and healthy differences of opinion as by agreement. Organisational contexts in which this is acknowledged and encouraged will help promote these aspects of partnership working.

No person, or agency, is an island in the provision of health and social care. Each is connected to the other and working together is essential in order to promote optimum outcomes for service users. Partners are not helped by undue dependence of any one on any other and none can act independently of the rest. The way forward is through recognition of the inter-dependence whereby each makes their unique contribution in such a way that benefits and enhances the whole.

Recommendations for good practice in partnership working

- As there is no 'senior partner' in most co-working there should be a co-operative willingness to put the needs of the service user at the centre of work undertaken.
- Conflict between partners should be acknowledged as a fact of life and appropriate mechanisms should be in place whereby differences can be addressed.
- Necessary policies should be established, together with the spirit of goodwill and compromise necessary to make them work.
- Partners should work with one another rather than against each other.

- The value of the 'container function' of partnership working at its best should be recognised, developed and harnessed.
- Partners should have forums whereby they talk and meet face-to-face.
- There should be opportunities for partners to see one another's places of work.
- Partners should record appreciation of each others input when this is indicated.
- Partners should be able to disagree as well as agree within the context of healthy debate.

CHAPTER 9

Customer satisfaction

This chapter begins with an acknowledgement of the increasing importance of eliciting views from service users (or customers) of health and social care in respect of the services they receive. Examples are given of customer satisfaction questionnaires and in-depth interviews and ways in which these have been modified and improved over time. Colleagues of EDTs are also shown to be service users. The extent to which EDTs can conduct their own enquiries into customer satisfaction and when these enquiries should be made by someone independent of the team is discussed and illustrated. The importance of such enquiries being culturally sensitive and promoting anti-oppressive practice is emphasised as are the ethical aspects of conducting enquiries. Consideration of how words can be turned into action along with an acknowledgement of the need for professionals to be open to challenge if they are to optimise their service delivery is shown. The chapter ends with some recommendations for good practice in obtaining customer feedback.

The emerging role of the customer in health and social care

While health workers have traditionally worked with patients, social workers used to refer to recipients of their services as clients. In more recent years the term 'service user' has found favour because it acknowledges that people sometimes do not have a choice about services they receive (for example in some mental health and child protection instances) and they are often using these public services, rather than paying for them as most clients normally would. Personal accounts from people suffering depression have provided valuable insights into the quality and effectiveness of services provided from the perspective of the service user, rather than provider (Plath, 1963; Wurtzel, 1995; Shaw, 1997). The first major study inquiring into service users' perceptions of social casework was published by Mayer and Timms (1970) and entitled *The Client Speaks*. In 1970 the notion of actually asking clients for their views and documenting these was considered to be ground-breaking. Essentially the suggestion was that clients might be seen as active contributors to service provision rather than being merely passive recipients of it. More recently there have been further studies inquiring into service users' perceptions of social care (see for example Rees, 1978; Smith, 1999b).

The need for service providers to be seen to consult with those who receive these services and take meaningful account of their views has been emphasised in recent government guidance relating to *best value* principles. Interestingly, the wording of this guidance moves away from using the term patient, client, or service user, and prefers *customer* instead:

> *A customer focus to reviews is essential. It is important that authorities seek out the views of all potential users, especially those who have traditionally been under-represented. Those that fail to engage local people fully from the outset – including hard-to-reach groups – will carry little conviction when it comes to explaining decisions on service targets and selected providers, and invariably overlook real opportunities to bring about lasting change.*
>
> (Department of the Environment, Transport and the Regions, 1999: 13)

Best value has four underlying principles – to challenge, compare, consult and compete. The consultation aspect of these principles is the particular focus of this chapter. Because EDTs frequently have only a single contact, rather than an ongoing relationship with many of their service users, these users constitute a 'previously under-represented and hard-to-reach' group. Even so, EDTs are not exempt from the need to consult with their customers. The first question this raises is who these customers are.

One EDT analysed the sources of their referrals over the course of a year. Out of 5,700 calls they found that:

- 27 per cent were received from daytime colleagues
- 23 per cent came direct from service users
- 23 per cent were from family, friends, carers, or neighbours of service users
- 11 per cent were from the police
- 9 per cent from health colleagues and
- 7 per cent other (eg district councils, other EDTs, women's refuges) (Smith and Muldoon, 2003).

EDTs therefore have several different types of customer (not counting students who also use their services – see Chapter 5). How can the various views of these different customers be sought and used in a meaningful way which helps to inform and enhance service provision?

Keeping the customer satisfied? Examples of satisfaction surveys

An initial attempt to ascertain service users' perceptions of the service they received was made in 1995 when 78 letters were sent out to people who had contacted EDT (for more detail see Smith, 2000a). In gaining the team members' agreement to, and co-operation with the survey, careful forethought and discussion was needed to ensure that it was seen by them as a genuine attempt to improve the service rather than a covert mechanism to check up on individuals.

Eighteen replies were received – a response rate of 23 per cent. The letter sent explained that the team was keen to improve the quality of their service where possible and that the opinions of those who had used these services would help them in this respect. Service users were asked:

1. *How long did you wait before your call was answered?*
2. *Did you find the social worker's response to your call: Very helpful?/Helpful?/Unhelpful?*
3. *With regard to the outcome of your contact with EDT were you: Very satisfied?/Satisfied?/ Dissatisfied?*
4. *Are there any comments you would like to make?*
5. *Would you be prepared to talk in more detail about your contact with EDT?*

A stamped addressed envelope was enclosed for completed forms to be returned. The EDT office address was not used as EDTs commonly do not want to attract visits from service users in person. The questions were formulated on the basis of what was known to be important for service users, namely that their calls were answered quickly and that they experienced the worker as responding to them in a helpful manner. A separate question was asked concerning the outcome of the call, distinguishing this from the response of the worker, as it was hoped that respondents to the brief questionnaire would recognise that there were limits to what an EDT worker could reasonably do for them. The response rate to this survey was too low to generalise from although generally high levels of satisfaction were reported at least from those having a realistic conception of what EDT could and could not do. One respondent expressed dissatisfaction with EDT because they did not remove his children from a care order and return them to him. Since this course of action was not within the gift of EDT at the time, the man's dissatisfaction needs to be acknowledged as being valid for him but as lying beyond the scope of what EDT could have done for him at the time.

Twelve respondents expressed a willingness to talk in more detail about their experience of the team and four of these were subsequently interviewed and recorded on audio-tape by EDT members. These interviews provided valuable material and an example of one respondent's experience (the mother of a disabled son) is given in Chapter 4. People are more likely to agree to participate in research if they think they might benefit from doing so. This mother felt very strongly that the provision available for her son was inadequate and that more should be available. She wanted to get her views across to the director of social services and following the interview a copy of the tape was given to the director who then listened to it. For senior officers flooded by paper work and electronic communications, audio tapes can make a welcome change, providing a useful method by which they can be briefed on matters of importance. This service user's view of EDT was astutely perceived and cogently expressed, 'I've always viewed EDT as if it was a bandage. If you cut your arm you would dress it with a bandage until you get to hospital to get it seen to properly – in other words until you can be seen by the daytime team'. This is an articulate statement of the remit of many EDTs (see Chapter 1).

A service user who frequently suffered episodes of manic depression talked of her contact with the team:

> I tend to 'phone EDT when I'm depressed or low. At those times I need someone to talk to me and reassure me that I'll be OK because I feel so low that I want to go and jump in the lake. I've never wanted to jump off a bridge – it's always the water for me as I find water calming. I ask myself, why have I had this illness? It makes me upset, as, on the whole, I'm a good person. I haven't been horrible or evil like some people. What I want from EDT is to be reassured that I'm OK and that nothing will happen to me because I get very frightened. I get afraid that people may be exploiting me or rip me off because when you've got mental illness you're very vulnerable. EDT workers can help me by using the right kind of words – a lot of love and nice words that show that I'll be OK until the morning when someone can come and see me. They help by being really positive, by encouraging me to relax when I'm feeling on edge and very panicky.

Like the previous service user quoted, this respondent shows an accurate understanding that the primary role of EDT is to help people through 'until the morning'. When listening to callers in mental distress EDT workers are motivated primarily by a pragmatic interest as to what *works* for the particular person to alleviate their pain. This insightful recognition of what this caller finds helpful acts almost as an instruction manual that she would like EDT workers to follow when responding to her. Like all callers, she knows herself better than any professional and is therefore well qualified to identify responses she would prefer in the first instance.

A constant dilemma for EDT workers engaged in assessing risks posed to service users and others is that of wondering whether talking alone will be sufficient or whether action needs to be taken. The service user spontaneously addresses this question:

> Sometimes speaking is enough but I remember one time when the EDT worker asked another care worker to visit me. She took me to hospital that night. I was beginning to feel unwell and didn't know how I would get through to the next morning. Once at hospital I felt safe although I know that it is not always a safe place to be in.

Once again, the emphasis is on getting through to the next morning. There is recognition that talking alone might not suffice at times and that action will prove necessary. This extract also illustrates the value of EDTs being able to call on appropriate additional staff at times of need. This service user was pleased to share her perceptions of EDT as she saw it as a way in which she could help them to help her most effectively. She also said that she had felt helped by the team previously and wanted to help them, in return, by giving them something they wanted and that she could give – her opinion of the service.

Customer satisfaction surveys are now routinely included in one EDT's annual report (Smith and Muldoon, 2003) and improvements have been made to the original design of the survey. With regard to the options that respondents were offered following questions two and three above, it was pointed out that three possibilities were offered; two favourable for EDT and one unfavourable. This creates a subtle loading in favour of EDT and more recent surveys have included four rather than three options, two favourable for EDT, two unfavourable. It was found that most people failing to return the questionnaire did not do so because of objecting to the survey or because they were unwilling to give their view but because they had forgotten about the form or not got around to completing it. Response rates in subsequent surveys were therefore increased relatively easily to 60 per cent or more by adding to the original letter, 'If we have not heard back from you within three weeks we will telephone you to see if you would prefer to give us your view then. Please let us know if you do not want us to do this.' On being telephoned most people were prepared to give their perceptions of the team's involvement with them.

Because a large proportion of EDT work is concerned with mental health service users it is likely that people might be mentally unwell when contacted about the survey. One service user who suffered from manic depression demanded to speak to the EDT manager insisting that she had not contacted the team on the date specified on the customer satisfaction letter. After several minutes of indignant annoyance she then calmed down and talked thoughtfully and insightfully about her experiences as a user of mental health services. Her comments provided valuable feedback both for EDT and for mental health services more generally.

The approach described thus far has involved EDTs carrying out surveys concerning their own work. This might raise objections that such surveys will inevitably lack independence and objectivity. One way of addressing this has been to ask the (independent) social services department comments and complaints officer to contact all those respondents who express willingness to talk in more detail about their contact with EDT.

In one year, out of 50 people originally surveyed, 21 said they would be prepared to talk in more detail about their contact with EDT. Names of these people were forwarded to the comments and complaints officer who contacted them to find that the circumstances of six had changed to the extent that they were no longer willing or able to participate in the follow-up study. She therefore conducted telephone interviews with the remaining 15. Feedback received was illustrative and frequently complimentary (the following quotations are taken from Smith and Muldoon, 2003: 17–19):

One client commented that EDT provided a life-saving service on one occasion. The client had called EDT after an episode of self harm, the emergency services were immediately called to her house and she received the help she needed. The client was impressed by the staff at EDT and their understanding of her problem, which had not always been taken seriously or understood by other services in the past.

One caller had made a series of calls to EDT regarding his girlfriend who had mental health problems. He found the advice given by EDT invaluable. His girlfriend was due to return to her home in another country for treatment but was too ill to board the flight.

> *Following a call to EDT before he left with his girlfriend for the airport, EDT telephoned the airport and discussed the best options for dealing with the situation. The caller felt that EDT staff were extremely helpful and valued their willingness to remain involved after the initial advice given.*

Unsurprisingly, not every caller was satisfied with every contact:

> *Three clients did not receive the help wanted. Of these one felt that her consultant psychiatrist was greater help as the advice given by EDT was not felt to be useful. Another client felt that EDT was unable to give her the help she needed because they were not fully informed of her situation and that the staff were unable to handle her call for help. She felt that a mental health worker should be on standby when the EDT service was open to callers and that a précis of vulnerable social services clients' notes should be available to EDT workers. She also believed that a greater level of mental health training would be of benefit to EDT staff. The client felt that each time she called EDT she had to give them the same information which did not help with the sometimes suicidal thoughts which troubled her.*
>
> *One client's perception of her involvement with EDT appears to have been completely negative. She had been a regular caller but did not feel that EDT was able to help her with her problems which seem to have been quite profound. This illustrates the dependence on EDT service users by clients with mental health problems outside regular working hours.*

Overall, however, the responses elicited about the work of the team were favourable:

> *The majority of those who discussed further their involvement with EDT clearly valued the service provided by the staff and their willingness to spend time listening to problems. The time that EDT staff were able to give to callers was an important factor for most callers. Even two of those who had said that they had not received the help they wanted from EDT said that they would use the service again, citing the helpfulness of the staff as a key factor. One of these callers recognised that EDT had given good advice although this had not ultimately helped in achieving a resolution to the problem. The second could not understand why EDT could not give the help they asked for but still felt that she would call again.*

As well as providing the team with useful feedback regarding its work these comments provide suggestions as to how the teams' responses could be improved. While it might not be possible to implement all suggestions made, it is right that a service intended to help those who contact it should be as sensitive as possible to what its recipients regard as effective help.

In recognition of the fact that fellow professionals are also users (customers) of the services that EDT provide satisfaction surveys have also been conducted seeking the views of daytime colleagues and partner agencies who refer to, and work with, the team. These colleagues have been asked to score the EDT on availability of worker, attitude, helpfulness, understanding effectiveness and feedback. Once again, provided that referrers have an accurate understanding of the limitations of EDT's role and resources they tend, generally, to indicate reasonably high levels of satisfaction. A recent survey of this kind showed that colleagues wanted more detailed feedback from EDT in response to their referrals and the team attempted to address this in their subsequent work.

Official complaints from service users are another type of feedback and these should be responded to appropriately and within acceptable timescales. Those complaining have frequently been unaware of the extent of EDTs remit, the size of the area they cover with minimal staffing levels and the few resources that are available to them. This ignorance has often provoked the complaint. Occasionally, but rarely, a worker's response may be found to have been inappropriate, and this needs to be addressed through line management and supervisory channels (see Chapter 7). EDTs hosting 'open days', contributing to road shows and carers' forums, in addition to providing publicity leaflets to potential referrers and users for display in main reception areas, are additional ways of promoting what they do and gaining feedback. Being interviewed by, and appropriately publicised in, local media, is another way in which teams can gain publicity and obtain feedback.

Over recent years EDT customer satisfaction surveys have been worded in accordance with local and national political initiatives and designed to generate material necessary for meeting performance indicators. Of particular importance has been the need to provide services which are culturally sensitive.

Cultural sensitivity and anti-oppressive practice

The first Social Services Inspectorate review of EDTs *Open all hours?* states, 'Emergency out of hours services (should) respond to the needs and preferences of service users, and services provided (should be) sensitive to race, religion, language, culture, gender and disability'. (Department of Health, 1999: 45). The following discussion focuses on the needs of African and Caribbean ethnic groups and provides an example of how service user feedback can be used to determine effective service provision. A similar process could also be followed for other discriminated against groups such as older or disabled people.

The *National Service Framework for Mental Health* (1999), 'Gave special emphasis to the cultural sensitivity of services for African and Caribbean ethnic groups, the assessment of Asian ethnic groups and the plight of socially excluded groups, such as refugees' (The Sainsbury Centre, 2002: 20). Black service users have long been over-represented in aspects of the mental health system. They are more likely to be detained by the police under suspicion of being mentally disordered and more likely to be treated with compulsion and medication once in psychiatric care (Browne, 1995; The Sainsbury Centre, 2002). Unfortunately, some fear that they will die as a consequence of being detained in police or psychiatric facilities and this fear is born of the tragic reality of deaths of black service users in care and custodial settings (The Sainsbury Centre, 2002: 21).

The pain and mistrust resulting from racism and oppression leads to the creation of 'circles of fear' whereby professionals fear black service users as 'the Other' (Fanon, 1986). Service users fear getting caught up in a system that will not understand them, will over-medicate them, and possibly kill them. Added to this, professionals frequently feel that they cannot talk about race openly and directly for fear of being thought or called racist as individuals, or working for organisations tainted and corrupted by institutional racism. With few effective outlets for these complex and interlinked fears they spiral around one another forming circles too tight for anyone to break, within which all become trapped (The Sainsbury Centre, 2002).

Fearing unsympathetic responses black service users often delay seeking help, and therefore are more likely to present to mental health services in acute crisis. Families and friends are reluctant to involve services fearing negative outcomes for the person they care for. Because of the crisis nature of many referrals, agencies such as the police have to take firm action, although they may be uncomfortable about doing so (The Sainsbury Centre, 2002: 27), and may thereby be seen as conforming to unpopular stereotypes.

It can be difficult for EDT workers dealing with black service users who have a history of depression and self-harm and who talk of wanting to harm themselves and/or others. These service users might refuse the offer of speaking to a covering doctor who does not know them for fear that they will be prescribed more medication that produces unwelcome side effects. This leaves the EDT worker in an uncomfortable position. Whilst recognising the possible validity of this fear and attempting to 'hold' the person's distress they also need to acknowledge that medical intervention might yet prove to be necessary in cases of serious mental illness. Once again, EDT workers are faced with the familiar dilemma – can the acknowledgement provided by appropriate listening and talking prove sufficient or should action be taken?

The Sainsbury Centre (2002: 69) recognise that professionals from white majority groups do not necessarily intend to discriminate in their responses, but point out that considerable powers of social control are invested in them and that this will inevitably influence how they are seen:

Even though professionals do not act in a deliberate way to oppress and marginalise Black people, they inevitably represent a system that gives them power to carry out these restricting and controlling duties. These controlling methods of work unfortunately reflect how Black people experience the world generally.

Addressing discrimination and oppression effectively is extremely difficult. The Sainsbury Centre (2002: 61, 72) recommend that:

- Agendas are client based, taking account of cultural needs and supporting carers and families.
- Strong partnerships are formed between statutory, voluntary, private and community organisations.

- Services are developed and rooted in the local community.
- Strong links are formed with local service user groups.
- Patients are treated as people in staff-user relationships.
- Black communities should have a key role in setting the service agenda.
- People need to be able to feel that it is okay to talk 'race' and mental illness.

It is apparent how many of these recommendations need the views of service users if they are to become a reality. Obtaining such information can itself, be problematic, particularly as many black service users resent being 'over-researched' and might be cynical about what differences expressing their views will really make. One very small step taken by one EDT wanting to provide the most culturally appropriate service they could was to add the following question to those asked in their customer satisfaction survey, 'Was there any way in which the person you spoke to could have been more sensitive to any social, cultural or religious issues important to you?' This represents a modest attempt to take the needs of these particular service users seriously and invites them to communicate more openly and specifically about race, culture and religion. Questions like this one might not be answered if the person believes that nothing will be done differently anyway. The extent to which respondents can reasonably expect to see changes in service provision as a direct result of their giving their views is one of several ethical aspects of eliciting feedback from service users.

Ethical aspects of canvassing views

An objection often raised about customer satisfaction surveys is that no good will follow from people giving their opinions, that no real changes will be made because organisations are interested primarily in conducting these surveys for their own purposes – to be seen to do the approved thing at the right time. This objection is particularly likely from groups such as the black service users, mentioned above, who regard themselves as being 'over-researched', constantly being told that their views are important, yet seeing no obvious benefit resulting from sharing these views. It is certainly easier to conduct such surveys than to make appropriate and lasting changes as a result of the findings. Even so, there can be gains in hearing from service users how they prefer to be treated – what *works* for them and how EDT workers can best help them access their own coping resources (see example above). 'Being heard' can, in itself, make a difference as one of the deepest needs of human beings is to be acknowledged, listened to and understood (Rogers, 1967; Covey, 1992).

Freud (1905: 224) provides an example of how being heard and responded to can be of benefit when writing of a three-year old boy, afraid of the dark, calling out to his aunt from a darkened room, 'Auntie, speak to me! I'm afraid because it's so dark.' His aunt answered him, 'What good would that do? You can't see me.' 'That doesn't matter' replied the child, 'if any one speaks, it gets light.' Calling out (speaking) and being listened to can illuminate emotional darkness and this illumination can open up further areas of thought and enquiry.

Whether or not someone else should be present when service users are being interviewed face-to-face merits thought. Although interviews might be tape recorded and subsequently transcribed there still remains the possibility of misunderstanding or misinterpretation of verbal and non-verbal communication (Smith, 1999c). If, throughout the process of being interviewed service users become distressed as a result of recalling distressing experiences, consideration should be given as to who they might turn to for help (Lee, 1993; Smith, 2002).

A further ethical aspect of conducting customer satisfaction surveys is whether or not service users should be paid or otherwise reimbursed for their time. Service providers can believe that users will be grateful for having their views sought so that they forget that the users are experts in their own right by virtue of the experiences they have encountered and the specialist perspective they possess. Reimbursing service users might be problematic, particularly if they are not able to receive money or other gifts without this affecting state benefits they are claiming. Nevertheless, further exploitation of already marginalised groups should be avoided when seeking the views of representatives of these groups.

So far, this discussion has identified two groups; one who provides services and which wants to obtain the views of another who uses these services. This entails a clear power-imbalance; between provider and user, seeker of opinions and responder. This need not be the case. Power can be distributed more equitably.

From obtaining opinions to action and joint authorship?

Service users might be given a more significant voice and become more influential in the shaping of the services they receive if they are able to participate in determining who works for these services. Residents of *The Cheshire Homes* and other residential establishments have long been involved in interviewing and selecting staff applying to work in these units. Service users must be consulted about recruitment and selection processes for the recently-launched three-year social work qualification. Some training courses will routinely include opportunities for service users to share their experiences of services they have received. The 'Post-qualifying award in child care' includes service user feedback as an essential component of its assessment.

Mary Barnes. Two Accounts of a Journey Through Madness (Barnes and Berke, 1991) describes Barne's regression into madness and subsequent emergence into sanity in R.D. Laing's Kingsley Hall community in the 1960s. The two authors of the book are Mary Barnes herself and her psychotherapist, Joseph Berke. Barnes is the primary author. Berke assists her in telling her story. A more contemporary example of this co-authorship is to be found in *Out of the Dark* (Caine and Royston, 2003). In this book Linda Caine, the primary author, recalls her childhood trauma and its subsequent impact on her adult life with the assistance of Robin Royston, her psychotherapist. In both of these illuminating works the service user tells their story with the assistance of the service provider. Neither book states whether it was user or provider who most wanted to tell the story but both identify the user as the primary author. This represents a shift from providers ascertaining and conveying views of users because the providers assist the users in telling the stories they want to tell. This entails a different way of thinking about service provision, one which is not focused mainly upon the meeting of targets and measures dictated by the government in performance assessment frameworks.

Holland (1995) has moved from writing about experiences to social action by way of what she calls *social action psychotherapy*. Describing her part in setting up a community and psychotherapy service with depressed women on a multiracial inner city estate she emphasises the need to challenge pre-conceived thinking about provider and user roles:

> *This work is disrespectful of existing professional boundaries in three senses. First, it challenges the vested, and anxiously protected, interests of the many distinct professional groups involved in community work. Second, it has been necessary to demystify the conceptual language of psychology and sociology . . . Finally, in attempting to use available services it has been evident that the welfare system condones the passive victim but criminalises those who are angry and assertive . . . It challenges the very notion that professional intervention is necessarily better informed and more beneficial than lay action . . . This challenge does not obliterate the idea that specialists of various kinds may provide essential services. It objects only to the claim by any group that they always, exclusively, know best.*
>
> (Holland, 1995: 142)

Having been part of the creation of this community service Holland worked with it through to its tenth birthday. An indication of the balance of power was that, as a psychologist, she was voted off the management committee by other members at various times over the ten year period!

Not everyone has the capacity or the gift to work alongside service users so that projects become first shared and then run by them in the way that Holland could. Nevertheless, her work is a testament to what can be done by having the necessary willingness to see situations with new eyes and to challenge pre-conceived notions of professionals' and users' roles. In emphasising the importance of challenge she is prescient of the government's call to local authorities:

> *Without the element of challenge there can be no effective review: it is the key to significant improvements in performance . . . Challenging why and how a service is provided requires a fundamental rethink, asking basic questions about the needs that each service is intended to address.*
>
> (Department of Environment, Transport and Regions, 1999: 15)

Recommendations for good practice in obtaining customer feedback

- Both surveys and in-depth interviews should be used to ascertain customer satisfaction.
- Attempts should be made to determine why some people do not respond to requests for feedback information.
- Colleagues should also be seen as 'service users' for research purposes.
- EDTs should conduct some enquiries themselves but arrange for others to be conducted by an independent person or agency.
- Performance assessment framework indicators should be considered when wording questions.
- A proactive approach should be adopted for obtaining responses to questionnaires.
- Roadshows, open days and use of the media should also be considered as ways of obtaining feedback from service users.
- There should be some gain identified for service users asked for their views.
- Thought should be given as to how to implement changes identified from the feedback.
- Enquiries should promote cultural sensitivity and anti-oppressive practice.
- Thought should be given to ethical aspects of conducting enquiries.
- Consideration of how to move from discussion to action should form part of eliciting opinions.

Conclusion

CHAPTER 10

Review: in the role of the parents

Where to now?

Drawing on John Bowlby's (1988) attachment theory and D.W. Winnicott's (1965) concept of the 'holding environment' this chapter begins with a review of previous chapters to show how frequently EDT workers find themselves cast into roles of parental figures. Findings from the far-reaching Climbie inquiry (Laming, 2003) with particular reference to EDTs are then considered. While Laming did not acknowledge the many years of experience, skills and expertise that exist within many EDTs and which contribute to keeping children safe, he does acknowledge the need to work flexibly and creatively. These are the hallmarks of EDT work and are demonstrated throughout this book. Comparison is made between the health, morale and well-being of many EDTs and daytime teams. The EDT worker's relatively reduced bureaucracy, increased autonomy and need to work in the present moment are highlighted as significant factors contributing to effective team functioning. EDTs have been compared with dinosaurs but it is reasoned that the wheel might be a preferable and more appropriate metaphor. The chapter ends by emphasising the valuable contribution that EDTs can make towards fulfilling the changing needs and expectations for health and social care provision in Britain as 9 to 5 becomes 24/7.

In the role of the parents: attachment and holding

It is apparent from Chapters 2, 3 and 4 how often EDT workers act in the role of parents for service users. In order to protect children in accordance with The Children Act 1989 it may be literally a case of finding substitute parents to care for children if their real parents or guardians are unable or unwilling to do so. It may be necessary for them to attend an interview conducted under The Police and Criminal Evidence Act 1984 as an 'appropriate adult' who can be seen to be performing the role of a good and caring parent with the best interests of their child being paramount. EDT workers might support and encourage foster carers who are experiencing difficulties in managing children placed with them. In this role they are providing a parenting function for these substitute parents. The care and control aspects of safe and responsible parenting are a prominent feature of the responses required for effective work with mental health service users. Chapter 8 considers how *partners* can work together within a pseudo-parental relationship for the benefit of those for whom they are jointly responsible.

Sometimes the parenting tasks performed are practical, such as helping service users who have lost their key to gain access to their property, enlisting help to fix appliances that have broken, facilitating access to emergency financial help when this proves necessary, and helping people get home from various parts of the country. On other occasions the parental aspects of EDT work resemble Bowlby's (1988: 11) description of the provision of the secure base and the availability of attachment figures:

> This brings me to a central feature of my concept of parenting – the provision . . . of a secure base from which a child or adolescent can make sorties into the outside world and to which he can return knowing for sure that he will be welcomed when he gets there, nourished physically and emotionally, comforted if distressed, reassured if frightened. In essence this role is one of being available, ready to respond when called upon to encourage and perhaps assist, but to intervene actively only when clearly necessary . . . Much of the time the role of the base is a waiting one but it is none the less vital for that.

Several EDT callers frequently contact the team as if to 'touch base'. They appear to know what they want from making contact and are also able to recognise whether or not they get it. Their tone of voice changes from its agitated distress and becomes more calm conveying, 'yes, *that's* what I wanted'. Bowlby identifies the cardinal importance of *availability* for those in distress, recognising that encouragement and assistance are required more frequently than actual intervention (this is borne out by the fact that EDTs deal with the vast majority of their callers over the telephone and do not need to see them face-to-face). He also stresses the crucial aspect of *waiting* which is a feature of much EDT work. Bowlby acknowledges that normally self-sufficient adults still need dependable attachment figures as well as children, particularly when their usual strength, capabilities and coping mechanisms are not available to them (see the case of the man asking for the brigadier in Chapter 4 and, more generally, in Aguilera 1998):

> Attachment behaviour is any form of behaviour that results in a person attaining or maintaining proximity to some other clearly identified individual who is conceived as better able to cope with the world. It is most obvious whenever the person is frightened, fatigued, or sick and is assuaged by comforting and caregiving . . . Whilst attachment behaviour is at its most obvious in early childhood, it can be observed throughout the life cycle, especially in emergencies.

(Bowlby 1988: 26)

When frightened and worried, people cast around for suitable attachment figures whom they perceive as being bigger, stronger, more knowledgeable, and better equipped to cope with the world than they are. EDTs perform this role in the minds of many service users who might regress at times of stress and crisis, feeling lonely and isolated in the darkness, and turn to them for help. On other occasions EDTs act as a projection post for those who have not enjoyed good parenting and who want someone to blame, hate or on whom they can vent their anger. Sometimes EDT workers will experience attacks from service users which seem out of all proportion to the situation or their role. Such attacks seem perplexing in the extreme but might be helpfully thought of as being essentially a deflection of the rage that a service user feels towards a parental figure whom they feel has let them down in the past. Some adult callers present with apparently insatiable hungers for love, approval and reassurance. When things go badly they might denigrate EDT workers because they are not consciously able or willing to hate their own parents or parental figures. The power and impact of such expressed emotions can be confounding. One female mental health service user, prone to repeated and serious self-harming episodes, sounded coldly sober when she told a male EDT worker, 'I need you to come around here and give me a good thrashing'.

Bowlby's attachment theory has relevance to EDT work because he emphasises the vital importance of availability, claiming that the fear of separation, being cut off from contact with necessary attachment figures, is the greatest fear of all, 'Threats to abandon are a degree more frightening to a child than threats no longer to love him' (Bowlby 1988: 147). At least EDTs are there, available, even if this entails callers having occasionally to wait for a response. By being available they fulfil an essential function that helps to promote better mental health in a population frightened and worried in the darkness. The knowledge that they are there might even be appreciated by those who do not go on to make contact with the team. Just knowing someone is there if needed is sometimes sufficient.

A question often asked by EDT workers is 'Can this situation *hold* until the next working day?' (see Laming, 2003: 49). The word 'hold' is a significant one for parents, and EDT workers acting in the role of parents, because both children and adults need holding, physically and mentally, in order to flourish. It is of interest that the word 'hold' derives from Germanic origins meaning 'watch and guard' (Ayto, 1990: 284) since watching and guarding are also functions of EDT workers on duty throughout the night (Smith and England, 1997). Ward (2001: 33) refers to D.W. Winnicott's (1965) concept of the 'holding environment' by which he meant:

> . . . the totality of the mother's provision for her young child . . . 'holding' goes well beyond literal physical holding and beyond the immediate reassurance that a warm cuddle can provide to a distressed child. It refers rather to the whole quality and importance of the human context in which the young child begins its developmental journey . . . 'Holding' includes the appropriate containment of anxiety which might mean communicating to the other person – 'Let's think about that anxiety together until you can find a way or an opportunity to manage it for yourself.

Chapter 8 of this book includes discussion of the importance of the 'containment' Ward refers to. His statement, 'Let's think about that anxiety together until you can find a way or an opportunity to manage it for yourself' encapsulates the stance of many EDT workers when talking with distressed, disorientated and worried service users. Chapters 5, 6 and 7 which consider how EDT staff are trained, managed and supported are of importance as Ward goes on to acknowledge that:

> The quality of the holding environment of staff is the main determinant of the quality of the holding environment that they can provide for clients . . . (and) . . . The quality of the holding environment of staff is mainly created by the form of organisation and by the process of management.

(Ward, 2001: 34)

EDT workers need to be, and feel, held themselves if they are to be able to effectively hold service users at times of distress. Unfortunately an opportunity to acknowledge and affirm the holding aspects of good parenting provided by many EDT workers was lost by the inquiry into the death of Victoria Climbie.

The aftermath of the Climbie inquiry

The Victoria Climbie inquiry (Laming, 2003) is one of the most comprehensive, detailed and potentially far-reaching examinations concerning the tragic death of a child since such inquiries began in Britain following the death of Maria Colwell in 1974. The Climbie inquiry ends with 108 recommendations and is unusual in commenting on the role of EDTs. Recommendation 47 states:

> The chief executive of each local authority with social services responsibilities must ensure that specialist services are available to respond to the needs of children and families 24 hours a day, seven days a week. The safeguarding of children should not be part of the responsibilities of general out-of-office-hours teams.

(Laming, 2003: 142)

In one sense the aim of this recommendation is laudable. It seeks to ensure that children are effectively protected, 'round the clock', from those who would harm them and that children do not suffer as a result of an inferior service provided (typically) by only a lone worker with a generic remit. The effective implementation of Laming's recommendation however, is problematic in the extreme. Daytime social work teams struggle with recruitment and retention issues to the extent that in some areas vacancies for qualified social workers are as high as 40 per cent. These vacancy rates are, 'hindering the modernisation process and the achievement of national targets for social care services' (Social Services Inspectorate, 2001: 59) and indicate extreme difficulties for services in covering nine (a.m.) to five (p.m.) hour periods, let alone to extend this cover to out of hours. Offices are frequently unable to recruit agency workers to social work roles and, despite increasing attempts to attract staff from overseas, vacancy rates still remain high.

There is, however, a wealth of experience in child protection work to be found in most EDTs. The Social Services Inspectorate comment, 'EDT staff were mainly experienced and long serving. Many were older and some had made their career in out of hours work'. Their concern was not that current EDTs were unable to work well in protecting people at a time of crisis but, 'We questioned where the next generation of EDT workers would come from, as existing workers begin to retire'. (Social Services Inspectorate, 1999: 3–4). Clifford and Williams (2002) have shown that EDTs typically include some of the most experienced and well-qualified social workers in the country. 'EDT workers have an average of 17 years' service and have no plans to move on' (Williams, 2003: 40).

Far from safeguarding children more effectively Williams fears that the implementation of Laming's recommendation 47 will deny children protection from a group of staff amongst those best placed to give it:

> *To remove from practice those who currently undertake significant numbers of risk assessments in child protection pathologises the victims of confusing systems. Assessments undertaken by EDT workers are neither better or worse than their daytime counterparts, but they are certainly different. Their focus is on what degree of risk can be managed until the next working day; their assessment is holistic . . . and, because of the 'emergency' nature of their work, (they) have developed over many years complex strategies for ensuring they do not leave vulnerable people at risk . . . I am not suggesting that out-of-hours teams remain unaltered by the Climbie findings – quite the opposite. The contention here is that the system that has managed crises after hours for nearly 30 years can contribute helpfully to the child protection debate only if it is included.*

> (Williams, 200: 41)

Laming (2003b: 13) contends that, '. . . a single member of (EDT) staff possibly with little or no experiences of services for children, is frequently expected to cover all social care needs with an authority'. While within some EDTs workers might have little or no experiences of services for children, this would be unusual and is by no means true for all. Many have years, and sometimes decades, of experience of working with children prior to joining EDTs and most EDT staff will attend some form of ongoing updating training in child protection (see Chapter 5). Some EDT staff actually provide such training. In one EDT half of the team had completed the recently launched post-qualifying award in child care. As a team, therefore, they had a higher percentage of recently trained workers than their daytime counterparts who carried high vacancy levels, were staffed primarily by agency workers or who could not release employed staff to study because of the need to give priority to court work. As Williams suggests, EDTs have much of value to contribute to the child protection debate.

Elsewhere Laming (2003b: 9, 12) identifies EDT-specific skills as being important:

> *The future lies with those managers who can demonstrate the capacity to work effectively across organisational boundaries. Such boundaries will always exist. Those able to operate flexibly need encouragement, in contrast to those who persist in working in isolation and making decisions alone . . . The joint training of staff and the sharing of budgets are likely*

to ensure an equality of desire and effort to make them work effectively ... Robust leadership must replace bureaucratic administration. The adherence to inward-looking processes must give way to more flexible deployment of staff and resources in the search for better results for children and families.

The skills of EDTs in working effectively and flexibly across organisational boundaries are apparent throughout this book and especially in Chapter 8. Advantages of joint training are highlighted in Chapter 5 and the flexible deployment of staff and resources in the search for better results for service users are demonstrated by EDTs across the country every night of the year. EDT workers value their autonomy, they are capable of 'robust leadership' in a context relatively free of bureaucratic administration. Rather than suggesting, as Laming does, that EDTs should be subsumed by daytime models of work, the extent to which daytime teams can learn from EDTs in terms of recruitment and retention of staff should be acknowledged and examined. Possible reasons for the relative endurance of EDT staff are considered in the following section.

Health, morale and well-being: let the day's own trouble be sufficient for the day

As daytime teams struggle to recruit and retain appropriate staff, EDTs remain reasonably well-staffed with fairly robust morale and with a more or less steady stream of interest from potential new workers. Why?

One of the major differences between EDTs and daytime teams is the relative freedom from bureaucratic demands enjoyed by EDT workers. While they have to record their involvement in any situation, because of the crisis nature of the work and the lack of administrative support while workers are on shift, this recording usually contains details only of crucially relevant aspects of decision making. There is not the time for the comprehensive in-putting of data into computer systems necessary to demonstrate that performance indicators are being met. For many daytime workers this is an increasing source of frustration invoking resentful feelings, articulated as 'this isn't what I came into social work to do'. Many workers feel that they have been betrayed because their 'psychological contract' with the work has not been honoured (Schofield, 2003). While the performance indicator culture might be said to have grown up as a result of information being insufficiently recorded and incompletely available in the past, many daytime workers currently find that disproportionate amounts of their time are spent recording and demonstrating the work at the expense of actually *doing* it (Schofield, 2003). It seems as if the life, heart, and soul are being choked out of social work.

By way of contrast EDT workers enjoy a sense of practising social work 'like it used to be'. They have a generic remit and are accessible directly to the public without the barriers and filters which characterise many daytime services, such as being referred to a community mental health team (typically done by a general practitioner to a team meeting). This is not a lament for a lost 'golden age' but a recognition that all human beings have certain basic needs and that these needs have not and do not change substantially whatever political fashions come and go.

Along with this reduced bureaucracy is the fact that EDT workers generally tend to appreciate their greater autonomy. While not being able to contact managers readily out of hours has disadvantages there are gains for the self-esteem of EDT workers who enjoy wrestling with, and overcoming, difficulties that initially looked impossibly overwhelming. To find one's way through a problem that at first seemed insurmountable contributes to job satisfaction of the most rewarding kind. As well as enjoying considerable autonomy compared to their daytime counterparts concerning *how* they work, EDT workers can also determine to a considerable extent *when* they work. Once a rota has been agreed upon one team member will frequently swap shifts with another in the light of changed circumstances. Because everyone gains from this flexibility there is likely to be considerable willingness on the part of team members to help one another achieve changes they would like to make as, they know that, they themselves are likely to benefit from such consideration at a later date. This flexible approach to working life means that EDT members can determine a work/life balance for themselves which daytime workers talk about frequently but can achieve only rarely.

However busy a particular shift has been it is psychologically extremely healthy to be able to leave for home only when all work undertaken has been passed on to other colleagues. Shredding notes compiled throughout the process of a busy shift can feel cathartic and cleansing. Although one sometimes leaves wondering what might happen to certain people in various circumstances, a shift should not be completed without a clear record of involvement being passed on to colleagues together with a clear indication of what needs still to be done.

The aims of EDT workers are very modest – in essence they are to get through safely to the next working day. Working with this main aim in mind over several years influences how one sees the world. Goals become very short term. The priority is to address what most needs addressing first; the urgent as opposed to the important. The focus is on the immediate in the knowledge that lots of 'immediates' make a future. Repeatedly responding to crises helps workers to recognise the crucial importance of the present moment, rather than lamenting the past or guessing the future. Brandon (2000: 143) highlights the under-recognised value of being in the present:

> . . . *most of us in the mental health professions, are much of the time, to a surprising extent, not fully aware of our actual present. Much of the content of our consciousness is remembering, speculating, planning . . . or carrying on a busy inner dialogue. More specifically we professionals . . . may be diagnosing, 'prognosing', planning our next intervention, wondering what time it's getting to be, etc. – we are only rarely being really open to our experience of self and other . . .*

Working in the present and attempting to help service users move forward one small step at a time, EDT workers subscribe to the truth repeated in addiction recovery programmes across the world and articulated in the gospel of Matthew chapter 6, verse 34, 'Therefore do not be anxious about tomorrow, for tomorrow will be anxious for itself. Let the day's own trouble be sufficient for the day.'

The problems encountered and grappled with by those working in health and social care on a daily basis, are huge; disease, poverty, oppression, inequalities, abuse, violence . . . It is easy for individuals to become demoralised and burnt-out (Aguilera, 1998) as they feel increasingly powerless in the face of these 'giants'. The EDT worker is in the privileged position of being able to consider with people how they can best get through the night, or survive the weekend. If they can help with this, they have done something worthwhile.

While the demands of daytime work necessitate a different approach to work from that adopted by EDT workers it might be instructive for those attempting to recruit and retain daytime workers to appreciate the value of reduced bureaucracy, increased autonomy and the satisfactions of achieving modest, short-term aims.

Despite providing a mostly safe and reasonably responsive service over many years EDT workers frequently feel threatened from those who perceive their functioning to be inadequate such as suggested in the Climbie inquiry and quoted above. This fear is now considered.

Dinosaurs or wheels?

When EDT workers meet at conferences and training events someone will soon come up with the metaphor of the dinosaur to describe EDTs. The comparison rests on the fact that the dinosaurs, although powerful and influential at a certain time in history, failed to adapt to a changing environment and so died out. Writing of recommendation 47 of the Climbie inquiry (see above), Williams (2003: 41) uses this metaphor implicitly in his claim that, 'So far EDTs have been ignored and if Laming's proposal is acted upon they will become *extinct*' (own emphasis added). EDT workers seem constantly to fear being replaced, taken over, discarded and pushed aside in favour of a more up-to-date model.

Against this fear, however, it should also be acknowledged that EDTs have survived intact for nearly thirty years, through many changes, and continue to provide a service that has evolved over time while retaining many core aspects of functioning. In some areas daytime services (such as the approved social worker rota) are being supplemented by EDT workers working additional hours because daytime teams cannot attract the necessary staff. (There must be a message here to organisations struggling with recruitment and retention!) In Hampshire's 'Social Services Direct' the out of hours role has been enhanced and elaborated to provide a three-tier response to crises, including EDT, and this model provides a possible blueprint for other areas wanting to extend their out of hours services for mental health and child protection (Winchester, 2003). Far from lumbering towards extinction this EDT has become even more appreciated. Their unique combination of skills has been augmented and developed to meet callers' needs more effectively.

EDTs have the day-to-day (night-to-night) knowledge of what problems are likely to arise out of hours and have developed a wealth of crisis-holding skills in the context of formal and informal networks when responding to these problems over the years. They therefore have valuable contributions to make to debates about out-of-hours service needs and provision.

At one EDT training day a suggestion was made that the metaphor of the wheel, rather than the dinosaur, was a more fitting one for EDTs. Wheels were first conceived many years ago and have undergone many changes and modifications since they were first designed. They now come in many designs, sizes and colours; they are adaptable and can perform various different functions according to what is needed. Wheels combine contemporary and historical functions as they are constantly being put to new uses although their basic form and function remain fundamentally unchanged. Although subject to constant modification, they are unlikely to be entirely replaced or superseded because they have a unique and irreplaceable function.

Conclusion: calling time on 9 to 5

In an article entitled *'Calling time on 9 to 5'* Winchester (2003) claims that the 24 hour culture is here to stay. The trend for people to expect more or less comprehensive services to be available to them more or less 'around the clock' has been a notable feature of recent years. By continuing to retain essentially their same basic staffing structures and levels EDTs have not really caught up with or caught on to the philosophy underlying this fundamental change in expectations and patterns of living. Nor has the necessary funding been available. Nevertheless, over the years they have demonstrated that they are able to provide a human, humane response to callers in distress even when 'nothing can be done' or provided. On countless occasions caller and worker have been able to think through a crisis together in an attempt to achieve the best resolution possible.

EDTs may not have access to the most up-to-date systems, or be the most slick, sophisticated, sexy, hi-tech operation in an organisation but they know the truth of Biestek's (1967: 135) contention that, 'All human beings have certain common basic needs: physical, emotional, intellectual, social and spiritual. In adverse circumstances these common needs are felt with a special poignancy'. EDTs can help people in crisis to access their own resources to meet these needs and, on the basis of many years experience of this work, could be a valuable resource for other services whose aims are similar. In the constantly changing world of increasing expectations for comprehensive health and social care services the unique and invaluable contribution which EDTs can make towards shaping the future should remain neither out of sight, nor out of mind.

References

Aguilera, D. (1998) *Crisis Intervention. Theory and Methodology.* 8th edn. London, Mosby.

Aldridge, D. (1998) *Suicide. The Tragedy of Helplessness.* London, Jessica Kingsley.

Alvarez, A. (1996) *Night.* London, Vintage.

Ayto, J. (1990) *Bloomsbury Dictionary of Word Origins.* London, Bloomsbury.

Bagley, C. and Ramsey, R. (1997) *Suicidal Behaviour in Adolescents and Adults.* Aldershot, Avebury.

Barnes, M. and Berke, J. (1991) *Mary Barnes. Two Accounts of a Journey Through Madness.* London, Free Association Books.

Beckett, C. (2002) Stepping Over The Threshold. *Professional Social Work.* July, 10–1.

Berne, E. (1975) *What Do You Say After You Say Hello?* London, Corgi.

Bibby, P. (1994) *Personal Safety for Social Workers.* Aldershot, Arena.

Biestek, F. (1967) *The Casework Relationship.* London, Unwin.

Biggs, S. (1993) *Understanding Ageing. Images, Attitudes and Professional Practice.* Maidenhead, Open University Press.

Bion, W. (1962) *Learning From Experience.* London, Heinemann.

Bowlby, J. (1988) *A Secure Base. Clinical Applications of Attachment Theory.* London, Routledge.

Braithwaite, R. (2001) *Managing Aggression.* London, Routledge.

Brandon, D. (2000) *Tao of Survival. Spirituality in Social Care and Counselling.* Birmingham, Venture Press.

Briere, J. (1992) *Child Abuse Trauma. Theory and Treatment of The Long Lasting Effects.* London, Sage.

Browne, D. (1995) Sectioning: The Black Experience, in Fernando, S. (Ed.) *Mental Health in a Multi-Ethnic Society. A Multi-Disciplinary Handbook.* London, Routledge.

Buyssen, H. (1996) *Traumatic Experiences of Nurses. When Your Profession Becomes a Nightmare.* London, Jessica Kingsley.

Caine, L. and Royston, R. (2003) *Out of the Dark. One Woman's Harrowing Journey to Discover Her Past.* Kent, BCA.

Carson, D. (1996) Risking Legal Repercussions, in Kemshall, H. and Pritchard, J. (Eds.) *Good Practice in Risk Assessment.* London, Jessica Kingsley.

Casement, P. (1985) *Learning From The Patient.* London, Routledge.

Cell, E. (1984) *Learning to Learn From Experience.* New York, Albany.

Cleaver, H., Unell, I. and Aldgate, J. (1999) *Children's Needs: Parenting Capacity. The Impact of Parental Mental Illness, Problem Alcohol and Drug Use, and Domestic Violence on Children's Development.* London, HMSO.

Clifford, D. and Williams, G. (2002) Important Yet Ignored: Problems of 'Expertise' in Emergency Duty Social Work. *British Journal of Social Work.* 32: 2, 201–16.

Coleman, J. and Hendry, L. (1999) *The Nature of Adolescence*. 3rd edn. London, Routledge.

Covey, S. (1992) *The Seven Habits of Highly Effective People. Powerful Lessons in Personal Change*. London, Simon and Schuster.

Dalrymple, J. and Burke, B. (1998) Developing Anti-Oppressive Practice Teaching. *Practice*. 10: 2, 25–35.

Debecker, G. (1997) *The Gift of Fear. Survival Signals That Protect Us From Violence*. London, Bloomsbury.

Department of Health (1991) *Child Abuse. A Study of Inquiry Reports 1980–1989*. London, HMSO.

Department of Health (1999a) *'Open All Hours?' Inspection of Local Authority Social Services Emergency Out of Hours Arrangements*. London, Department of Health.

Department of Health (1999b) *Working Together to Safeguard Children*. London, HMSO.

Department of Health (2000) *The Framework for The Assessment of Children in Need and Their Families*. London, HMSO.

Department of Health (2001) *Modern Social Services: A Commitment to Deliver*. London, HMSO.

Department of Health (2002) *Suicide Prevention Strategy*. www.Doh.Gov.Uk.

Department of The Environment, Transport and The Regions (1999) *Implementing Best Value – A Consultation Paper on Draft Guidance*. London, HMSO.

Erikson, E. (1951) *Childhood and Society*. 1981 Edition. London, Triad/Granada.

Erikson, E. (1968) *Identity, Youth and Crisis*. London, Faber and Faber.

Etherington, S. and Parker, C. (1984) *Out of Hours Social Work. Report of A BASW Research Study*. Birmingham, BASW Publications.

Fanon, F. (1986) *Black Skin, White Masks*. London, Pluto Press.

Freud, S. (1905) *Three Essays on The Theory of Sexuality*. 1953 edn. London, Hogarth Press.

Freud, S. (1930) *Civilisation and Its Discontents*. London, Hogarth Press, 1961 edn.

Garland, C. (1998) *Understanding Trauma. A Psychoanalytical Approach*. London, Duckworth.

Garratt, P. (1999) Mapping Child-Care Social Work in The Final Years of The Twentieth Century. *British Journal of Social Work*. 29: 1, 27–47.

Goffman, E. (1957) *The Presentation of Self in Everyday Life*. 1978 edn. Harmondsworth, Penguin.

Hawton, K. (1986) *Suicide and Attempted Suicide Among Children and Adolescents*. London, Sage.

Hird, M. and Cash, K. (2000) Power Play. *Open Mind*. January/February.

Hodgkinson, P. and Stewart, M. (1991) *Coping With Catastrophe*. London, Routledge.

Holland, S. (1995) Interaction in Women's Mental Health and Neighbourhood Development, in Fernando, S. (Ed.) *Mental Health in A Multi-Ethnic Society*. London, Routledge.

Hughes, B. (1995) *Older People and Community Care. Critical Theory and Practice*. Maidenhead, Open University Press.

Hughes, L. and Pengelly, P. (1998) *Staff Supervision in a Turbulent Environment. Managing Process and Task in Front-Line Services*. London, Jessica Kingsley.

Issitt, M. (1999) Anti-Oppressive Reflective Practice and Multi-Disciplinary Working. *Journal of Practice Teaching*. 2: 2, 21–36.

Ives, C. (1997) The Mask of Self, in Jennings, S. (Ed.) *Dramatherapy: Theory and Practice, Volume 3*. London, Routledge.

Jack, G. (2000) Ecological Influences on Parenting and Child Development. *British Journal of Social Work*. 30: 6, 703–20.

Jamieson, A., Harper, S. and Victor, C. (Eds.) (1997) *Critical Approaches to Ageing and Later Life.* Maidenhead, Open University Press.
Jamison, K. (2000) *Night Falls Fast. Understanding Suicide.* London, Picador.
Johnstone, K. (1993) *Impro. Improvisation and The Theatre.* London, Methuen.
Jones, R. (2002) *Mental Health Act Manual. Eighth Edition.* London, Sweet and Maxwell.
Kempe, R. and Kempe, C. (1978) *Child Abuse.* London, Open Books.
Kemshall, H. and Pritchard, J. (Eds.) (1996) *Good Practice in Risk Assessment and Risk Management.* London, Jessica Kingsley.
Kemshall, H. and Pritchard, J. (Eds.) (1997) *Good Practice in Risk Assessment and Risk Management 2. Protection, Rights and Responsibilities.* London, Jessica Kingsley.
Kitwood, T. (1997) *Dementia Reconsidered. The Person Comes First.* Maidenhead, Open University Press.
Kobasa, S. (1982) The Hardy Personality, in Sanders, G. and Suls, J. (Eds.) *Social Psychology of Health and Illness.* New Jersey, Lawrence Erlbaum.
Kolb, D. (1984) *Experiential Learning: Experience as the Source of Learning and Development.* Englewood Cliffs, Prentice Hall.
Laming, H. (2003) *The Victoria Climbie Inquiry.* Norwich, The Stationery Office.
Laming, H. (2003b) *The Victoria Climbie Inquiry. Summary and Recommendations.* Norwich, TSO.
Lee, R. (1993) *Doing Research on Sensitive Topics.* London, Sage.
Levin, A. and Sheridan, M. (Eds.) (1995) *Munchausen Syndrome by Proxy: Issues in Diagnosis and Treatment.* London, Lexington.
Littlechild, B. (1996) *The Police and Criminal Evidence Act 1984. The Role of the Appropriate Adult.* Birmingham, BASW/Venture Press.
London Borough of Brent (1985) *The Report of The Panel of Inquiry Into the Circumstances Surrounding the Death of Jasmine Beckford.* London, Kingswood Press.
Mace, N. et al. (1985) *The 36-Hour Day. Caring at Home for Confused Elderly People.* London, Hodder and Stoughton.
Martin, P. (2002) *Counting Sheep. The Science and Pleasures of Sleep and Dreams.* London, Harper Collins.
Mason, T. and Chandley, M. (2001) *Managing Violence and Aggression. A Manual for Nurses and Health Care Workers.* Edingburgh, Churchill Livingstone.
Mayer, J. and Timms, N. (1970) *The Client Speaks. Working Class Impressions of Casework.* London, Routledge and Kegan Paul.
Meyerson, S. (Ed.) (1975) *Adolesence and Breakdown.* London, George Allen and Unwin.
Norris, D. (1990) *Violence Against Social Workers. The Implications for Practice.* London, Jessica Kingsley.
O'Hagan, K. (1986) *Crisis Intervention in Social Services.* London, BASW/Macmillan.
Obholzer, A. and Roberts, V. (1994) *The Unconscious at Work.* London, Routledge.
Offshe, R. and Watters, E. (1995) *Making Monsters: False Memories, Psychotherapy and Sexual Hysteria.* London, Andre Deutsch.
Plath, S. (1963) *The Bell Jar.* London, Faber and Faber.
Porter, R. (2002) *Madness. A Brief History.* Oxford University Press.
Preston-Shoot, M. (1995) Assessing Anti-oppressive Practice. *Social Work Education.* 14: 2, 11–29.
Rajaratnam, S. and Arendt, J. (2001) Health in A 24-H Society. *The Lancet.* 358: 999–1005.

Rees, S. (1978) *Social Work Face to Face*. London, Edward Arnold.

Ritchie, J., Dick, D. and Lingham, R. (1994) *The Report of The Inquiry Into the Care and Treatment of Christopher Clunis*. London, HMSO.

Rogers, C. (1967) *On Becoming a Person. A Therapist's View of Psychotherapy*. London, Constable.

Rustin, M. et al. (Eds.) (1997) *Psychotic States in Children*. London, Duckworth.

Rutter, M. and Rutter, M. (1993) *Developing Minds*. Harmondsworth, Penguin.

Schofield, P. (2003) 'It Doesn't Add Up . . .' *Community Care*. 24–30 April, 32–3.

Schon, D. (1983) *The Reflective Practitioner. How Professionals Think in Action*. Aldershot, Ashgate.

Shaw, F. (1997) *Out of Me*. London, Penguin.

Sheppard, M. (1990) *The Role of the Approved Social Worker*. Sheffield, Community Care.

Sinason, V. (Ed.) (1994) *Treating Survivors of Satanist Abuse*. London, Routledge.

Smith, M. (1999a) Learning Collectively to Collectively Learn: Training for Emergency Duty Teams. *Practice*. 11: 3, 5–14.

Smith, M. (1999b) Telling it Like it Was. Audio-Taping Stories Told by Mental Health Service Users and Carers. *Social Work Education*. 18: 4, 479–86.

Smith, M. (1999c) Researching Social Workers' Experiences of Fear. Piloting a Course. *Social Work Education*. 18: 3, 347–54.

Smith, M. (2000a) Keeping The Customer Satisfied? Service Users' Perceptions of an Emergency Duty Team. *Practice*. 12: 3, 39–48.

Smith, M. (2000b) Supervision of Fear in Social Work. A Re-Evaluation of Reassurance. *Journal of Social Work Practice*. 14: 1, 17–26.

Smith, M. (2001a) Risk Assessment in Mental Health Work. *Practice*. 13: 2, 21–30.

Smith, M. (2001b) The Framework for the Assessment of Children in Need and Their Families: Implications for Emergency Duty Teams. *Practice*. 13: 4, 39–48.

Smith, M. (2002) Half in Love With Easeful Death? Social Work With Adolescents Who Harm Themselves. *Journal of Social Work Practice*. 16: 1, 55–66.

Smith, M. and England, J. (1997) The Nightwatch and The Morning After: Experiences of Working for an Emergency Duty Team. *Practice*. 9: 3, 27–34.

Smith, M., Moody, C., Waterhouse, J. and Dell, P. (1998) Practice Teaching in the Dark: Student Placements at an Emergency Duty Team. *Practice*. 10: 2, 61–9.

Smith, M. and Muldoon, A. (2003) *EDT Annual Report 2002–2003*. Buckinghamshire County Council.

Smith, M. and Nursten, J. (1995) Murder, Suicide and Violence. Impacts on The Social Worker. *Journal of Social Work Practice*. 9: 1, 15–22.

Smith, M. and Nursten, J. (1998) Social Workers' Experience of Distress: Moving Towards Change? *British Journal of Social Work*. 28: 3, 351–68.

Social Exclusion Unit (2002) *Young Runaways*. London, Social Exclusion Unit.

Social Services Inspectorate for Wales (2001) *Inspection of Local Authority Social Services Out-Of-Hours Emergency Duty Service*. Social Services Inspectorate for Wales.

Taylor, B. (2000) *Reflective Practice. A Guide for Nurses and Midwives*. Milton Keynes, Open University Press.

Taylor, I. (1996) Facilitating Reflective Learning, in Gould, N. and Taylor, I. (Eds.) *Reflective Learning for Social Work*. Aldershot, Ashgate.

The Health and Safety Executive (1998) *Five Steps to Risk Assessment.* Suffolk, The Health and Safety Executive.

The Sainsbury Centre (2002) *Breaking The Circles of Fear. A Review of the Relationship Between Mental Health Services and African and Caribbean Communities.* London, The Sainsbury Centre.

The Social Services Inspectorate (2001) *Detained.* London, HMSO.

Thompson, N. (1991) *Crisis Intervention Revisited.* Birmingham, Pepar.

Thompson, N. (1993) *Anti-Discriminatory Practice.* London, Macmillan.

Thompson, N. (2002) *People Skills.* 2nd edn. Hampshire, Palgrave/Macmillan.

Vaughan, P. (1995) *Suicide Prevention.* Birmingham, Pepar.

Ward, A. (2001) Theory for Practice in Therapeutic Family Centres, in Mcmahon, L. and Ward, A. (Eds.) *Helping Families in Family Centres. Working at Therapeutic Practice.* London, Jessica Kingsley.

Williams, G. (2003) Night Caretakers. *Community Care.* 1–7 May, 40–1.

Williams, M. (1997) *Parents, Children and Social Workers. Working in Partnership Under The Children's Act 1989.* Aldershot, Avebury.

Winchester, R. (2003) Calling Time on 9 to 5. *Community Care.* 17–23 April, 28–30.

Winnicott, D.W. (1965) *The Maturational Processes and The Facilitating Environment.* London, Hogarth Press.

Wurtzel, E. (1995) *Prozac Nation. Young and Depressed in America.* London, Quartet.

Yelloly, M. and Henkel, M. (Eds.) (1995) *Learning and Teaching in Social Work: Towards Reflective Practice.* London, Jessica Kingsley.